Business-Focused

HR

11 Processes to Drive Results

Business-Focused HR

11 Processes to Drive Results

SCOTT P. MONDORE   SHANE S. DOUTHITT   MARISA A. CARSON

Society for Human Resource Management
Alexandria, Virginia
www.shrm.org

Strategic Human Resource Management India
Mumbai, India
www.shrmindia.org

Society for Human Resource Management
Haidian District Beijing, China
www.shrm.org/cn

This book is published by the Society for Human Resource Management (SHRM®). The interpretations, conclusions, and recommendations in this book are those of the authors and do not necessarily represent those of SHRM.

The Society for Human Resource Management (SHRM) is the world's largest association devoted to human resource management. Representing more than 250,000 members in over 140 countries, the Society serves the needs of HR professionals and advances the interests of the HR profession. Founded in 1948, SHRM has more than 575 affiliated chapters within the United States and subsidiary offices in China and India. Visit SHRM Online at www.shrm.org.

Cover design by: Shirley E.M. Raybuck
Interior design by: Shirley E.M. Raybuck

Library of Congress Cataloging-in-Publication Data

Mondore, Scott P.
Business-focused HR : 11 processes to drive results / by Scott P. Mondore, Shane S. Douthitt, and Marisa A. Carson.
     p. cm.
Includes bibliographical references and index.
ISBN 978-1-58644-204-0
1. Human capital. 2. Personnel management. 3. Success in business. I. Douthitt, Shane S. II. Carson, Marisa A. III. Title. IV. Title: Business-focused human resources.
HD4904.7.M65 2011
658.3--dc22

11-0171   2011013127

Contents

Foreword

Baptist Health Care embarked on a journey over 15 years ago to improve our health system with the ultimate goal of becoming the best health care organization in the country. Our results speak for themselves. We were honored to win the Malcolm Baldrige Award in 2003; we consistently achieve the 99th percentile in patient satisfaction compared to our competition; and we were named one of *Fortune* magazine's Best Places to Work for six years straight. In the midst of the worst economic meltdown since the Great Depression in 2009, we had our strongest financial year — ever. It was not one person or small group of senior leaders who made this happen. The key to sustaining our success has been our people, a focused and engaged workforce that helped us achieve these remarkable results and sustain them for well over a decade. Our five pillars are the foundation of everything we do: People, Service, Quality, Financial, and Growth, with People first — always.

Believing that people are important to your business, though, is not enough. When it comes to day-to-day execution, you must have HR processes that are aligned to your business strategy, have proven impact, and most importantly, have the buy-in of all your leaders. *Business-Focused HR* provides the practical roadmap to show leaders how to build, execute, and demonstrate the impact that HR processes have on business outcomes.

I am excited that the Society for Human Resource Management (SHRM) has asked the authors to write this book. It will have a great impact on organizations across industries. By following the authors' advice and implementing their practical approaches, CEOs can call upon human resources to act as a true business partner and drive outcomes, instead of being simply a support function or cost-center. Senior HR leaders will be able to show the return on investment of the processes they implement and demonstrate the direct alignment of their work to the business strategy. Front-line HR leaders will be able to execute these processes on a local level more easily since managers want processes that can be shown to impact their key performance metrics. Other "C-suite" leaders will look to human resources as a partner that they can work with cross-functionally to help them reach their performance goals.

The authors' significant research background and expertise lends credibility to the applied research focus of the book, and the evidence-based processes it introduces to the reader.

Business-Focused HR is an important work. The authors share their experiences and expertise gained through assisting some of the most respected companies in the country in building great HR processes and functions. Whether you are a *Fortune* 50 corporation, a small business, or a community-based health system like us, you will benefit from their direct, practical advice.

Understanding that people truly drive outcomes is so important in creating a positive culture that produces results. However, effective and aligned HR processes, with proven value and impact, will sustain your success into the future.

Al Stubblefield
President/CEO, Baptist Health Care
Pensacola, Florida

Preface

Having worked inside and outside human resources throughout our careers — in operations, strategy, and sales, and even as CEOs turning around entire organizations — it is always exciting for us to see a strong focus on people being the true drivers of business decisions — rather than a short-term focus on market share or stock price. HR practitioners have demanding jobs that are sometimes rewarding (sometimes not), but they are always critical because they are responsible for their organizations' most essential assets. Unfortunately, even today, some leaders still fail to see the value that human resources delivers. At the Society for Human Resource Management's 2009 Annual Conference, Jack Welch noted that HR managers have the most significant job in America; however, our value is often overlooked by those outside human resources. As much as we would like to blame those other leaders for not seeing the light, perhaps the responsibility lies with HR practitioners for not properly demonstrating their value and aligning what they do with business outcomes. In our first book, *Investing in What Matters: Linking Employees to Business Outcomes*,[1] we introduced a practical process to link people data directly to business results. The overarching theme of that book was to teach leaders how to build an HR strategy that is data-driven and evidence-based and has a calculated return on investment (ROI). That process is very much alive here in *Business-Focused HR*, but we understand that to make the process actionable, this process needs to be illustrated for individual HR processes. SHRM encouraged us, through the publication of this book, to document how we have turned key HR processes into business-focused initiatives using these approaches, tools, and tactics. To that end, we have included 11 core HR processes in this book.

The stakes remain the same for organizations and HR leaders, whether we are in a booming or lagging economy — HR professionals must show the value of what they do and build a compelling business case to get other, potentially skeptical, leaders to buy in. This book will provide the tools for HR leaders and people managers across the organization to become more business-focused with the processes that they execute. Senior HR leaders can make the business case to top management, while front-line practitioners can demonstrate the value of what they do to managers on the "shop-room floor." Having a practical resource that takes HR leaders step-by-step through what the latest research tells us, from best practices in execution to linking the process directly to business outcomes, is our goal. Ultimately, the aim is for *Business-Focused HR* to become the guidebook for all HR leaders to enable them to become strategic business partners at all levels and across all functions in their organizations.

Core HR Processes and Chapter Overviews

The 11 core HR processes/topics selected for exploration include everything from employee opinion surveys and employee selection to "hot" HR topics, such as succession planning and work/life balance. We conclude with a chapter that gives practical advice on creating a business-focused HR scorecard and additional applications of the approaches applied in the book. A brief overview of each chapter is provided below.

Chapter 1. HR Processes and Business Outcomes

The HR function has made great strides to align itself more effectively with the business strategy and key stakeholders across the organization. However, gaps still remain in (1) how human resources shows the direct connection between what HR practitioners do every day and meaningful business outcomes, and (2) the integration of existing research with HR practitioners' approach to executing core processes. This chapter reviews these issues and introduces a clear and practical approach to bringing the information and data together (the Business Partner RoadMap™) to draw meaningful conclusions about the impact of HR processes on business outcomes. This process allows HR leaders to develop a business-focused strategy and to demonstrate the business value of 11 different HR processes.

Chapter 2. Employee Selection

Numerous organizations still hire people by committee — allowing multiple managers to conduct unstructured interviews and then make a "consensus" decision on candidates. This chapter will take you through the research on the myriad of selection techniques at your disposal — and their overall validity and effectiveness. Using a case study, we will take you from start to finish on selecting the right hiring techniques for your organization, gaining managerial buy-in, minimizing legal risk, and maximizing the number of quality hires. We will also show you how to calculate the ROI and overall effectiveness of your current selection tools and the expected ROI of the tools that you may decide to use in the future.

Chapter 3. Competency Models

Although competency models have become popular in organizations, they are often relegated to the status of "HR activities" that ultimately end up stored in file cabinets with little usage or impact on your business. The obstacles here continue to be centered on using the models as a foundation for HR strategies and on demonstrating the business impact of these competency models. This chapter will show you, with a case study, how to best use competency models and how to link competency ratings to job performance and other critical business outcomes.

Chapter 4. Performance Management

Performance appraisals have, unfortunately, become a dreaded yearly activity in many organizations, which is a problem because they represent a great opportunity to have a positive impact on employees and organizations. This chapter will show you, with a case study, how to build appraisals that are based on valid performance criteria, competencies, skills, and behaviors, and how to incorporate career development discussions into the process. We also show how to demonstrate the connection between competency ratings and business outcomes, thus transforming performance management from a "paper job" to a critical activity that drives the business.

Chapter 5. Multi-rater/360 Assessments

Multi-rater assessments are typically used to enhance individual development. However, opportunities exist in key areas to use multi-rater data to drive broad changes in organizations. This chapter will show you how to examine multi-rater data systematically, linking the competencies that are rated to business outcomes and analyzing all the data to identify systemic strengths and weaknesses.

Chapter 6. Employee Opinion Surveys

Conducting employee opinion surveys has become standard practice for many organizations, and while technology has made them cost-effective to execute, few organizations leverage the data collected to its fullest advantage. In this chapter, we provide the best approaches and tools for gaining senior and front-line leader buy-in and for executing the survey process. We demonstrate, with a case study, how competitive advantage is realized when organizations (1) involve senior leaders in the development of the survey tool, (2) create local and systemic initiatives, and

(3) create reports for all leaders that show exactly where they need to focus, based on level of impact on business outcomes.

Chapter 7. Employee Training

Organizations spend vast amounts of money to train their employees and often assume that the more money spent, the greater the impact. This chapter will provide you with the tools to determine, across your myriad of training programs, exactly which ones are driving outcomes and which have the potential to be cut. From this new vantage point, you will be able to refine your training strategy and properly calculate a return on investment (ROI). A case study will be used to demonstrate the process.

Chapter 8. Career Development

Focusing on employee career development helps organizations grow their pipeline of leadership strength, retain high-performing and high-potential staff, and develop needed skills and experiences among your employee population. This chapter will provide you with a straightforward approach to assessing what you need to know about your people (for example, their values, interests, and experiences) to get them on the right career path, as well as present research from across generations to help customize your approach. Further, we will show you how to make the business case for implementing this process in your organization and reveal a helpful tool to make the journey efficient and effective.

Chapter 9. Leadership Development

Leadership development can take numerous forms in organizations — and too many times it is driven by the latest consultant fads. The key to gaining competitive advantages with leadership development is to effectively diagnose who needs these programs and where the focus of these programs should be. This chapter will outline a process for competently executing and assessing leadership development initiatives and using them to drive business outcomes.

Chapter 10. Succession Planning

Succession planning is often referred to as more of an "art than a science"; however, enhancing the scientific part of the equation will bring your process more in-line with business goals and outcomes and help garner senior-level buy-in. This chapter will provide you with a process to quantify the impact of your current succession planning process and the quality of your talent pool, while allowing you to put your focus solely on the aspects that are pertinent to the business. A succession planning scorecard is provided to show you how to have the most impact at the senior level when planning your next talent moves.

Chapter 11. Work/Life Balance

Although work/life balance programs are offered in more and more organizations, very little is known about the impact these programs have on individuals and business outcomes. There is much assumed value, but little hard, confirmatory data. We review the research to discover the various possibilities for these programs. This chapter will show you how to effectively execute work/life balance or flexibility programs by assessing the level of need for them in your organization, implementing the right programs, and demonstrating the individual and organizational impact and value of the programs.

Chapter 12. Creating a Business-Focused HR Scorecard

The typical HR scorecard focuses almost exclusively on internal efficiency metrics (for example, time to hire) — which will limit the impact of the scorecard to human resources only. This chapter will introduce you to a four-step process that will incorporate many of the analytic techniques described throughout the book and will allow you to create an HR scorecard containing people metrics and initiatives that have been shown to have a cause-effect impact on business outcomes. Incorporating these known drivers of business outcomes will increase buy-in from all levels across the organization.

Chapter 13. Bringing It All Together: Next Steps and Opportunities

While a handbook cannot cover all topics in human resources, we will review the overarching themes that tie all the chapters together and discuss what is next for HR leaders. Finally, we present opportunities to use the techniques and tools offered in other areas within human resources and, importantly, beyond human resources as well.

Appendix A: Data Analytics

The appendix is designed to give additional tools and background information to get you started as quickly as possible in implementing any of these business-focused HR processes. This appendix will provide more detailed background around how to effectively put the Business Partner Roadmap™ into action — including key stakeholder interview questions and sample meeting agendas. It also includes some of the more statistical-related details and concepts that are discussed in the book — from reliability/validity to using structural equation modeling.

Appendix B: Reliability and Validity

In this appendix we provide additional details regarding the validity and reliability of your HR measures and metrics. In particular, we discuss content validity, discriminant validity, criterion-related validity, and reliability. As we will discuss, ensuring the validity and reliability of your measures (for example, multi-rater assessment and the employee opinion survey) is essential for scientific, legal, and practical reasons.

Chapter Content for Each HR Process

In order to accomplish the goals of this book, each chapter will focus on a single key HR process, describing (1) where it has been and where it is today, (2) how it is best executed to lead people based on applied research and practical experience, and (3) how to make the HR process more business-focused. We will briefly review some of the historical research in our field not only because it gives us an opportunity to see how the thinking has evolved (i.e. learning history so we do not repeat any mistakes) but also because many of the seminal or "classic" studies still guide us in making the right decisions when we build our processes and initiatives. Research that is done properly and that informs our thinking in a positive direction has no shelf life.

Each chapter will include the following:

What the Research Tells Us

» A short history of the HR process and how it has impacted our approach to leading people in organizations

» A high-level overview of study findings and what they mean in practical terms for HR business partners

Effective Design and Execution

» How to integrate the execution of the core HR process with the steps of the Business Partner RoadMap™

» Practical tips for effective execution from start to finish, with tips on presenting the case to CEOs, making HR processes useful for front-line managers, and overcoming barriers

Building a Business-Focused HR Process

» How to link the HR process to business outcomes

» How to show a return on investment

» A case study with linkage analysis and an example of how to determine where to make investments

CHAPTER 1

HR Processes and Business Outcomes

Over the years, organizations have steadily improved the overall implementation of numerous HR processes. These improvements are apparent in many ways, from the manner in which organizations execute the hiring and development of employees to the implementation of company-wide opinion surveys. However, organizations and HR functions often come up short, specifically in these key areas:

- Building the business case for HR initiatives
- Effectively executing HR initiatives from start to finish by applying proven best practices
- Demonstrating the cause-and-effect relationships between HR initiatives and business outcomes
- Calculating expected return on investment (ROI)
- Creating a culture of measurement and modification

These five key areas represent significant opportunities for HR leaders to confront, overcome, and leverage for competitive advantage. This book is the step-by-step guide HR practitioners need in order to incorporate best practices and fully leverage data and senior-leadership buy-in, across numerous HR initiatives, to drive business outcomes in their organizations. HR initiatives (and human resources, in general) should have a demonstrated impact on business outcomes, particularly in the current economy in which any opportunity to gain a competitive advantage is critical. At the same time, the outsourcing of human resources is becoming a real proposition; therefore, showing a definitive connection between what we do as HR leaders and how it impacts business results will help keep the function relevant in organizations and improve our professional standing. Human resources typically has a great reputation as a function that gets things done; it is now necessary to take the next step and show the true impact of all our hard work.

Incorporating the steps outlined in this book will enable HR leaders to be considered business partners and trusted advisors. The constant desire by HR leaders to be given a "seat at the table" has been hindered by our inability to demonstrate the value of HR initiatives in terms of their impact on bottom-line business results. The process outlined in this book will allow you to demonstrate meaningful and measureable value and impact the health, stability, and growth of the organization while also providing direction to the leadership team on how to execute effectively.

The Science-Practice Gaps

Let us start with a quick story: Every year we, as scientists-practitioners, attend the annual conference for the Society for Industrial and Organizational Psychology (SIOP). SIOP is a division of the American Psychological Association (APA) dedicated to industrial-organizational (I-O) psychology. In case you are not familiar with this discipline, it is basically the scientific study of the workplace where methods of psychology are applied to issues of critical relevance to business. The point is not to educate you on the field of I-O psychology but rather to highlight a key issue we talk about every year at the conference. For nearly 15 years, we have attended this annual conference and for most of those years, the content has focused on "closing the scientist-practitioner gap." This topic is discussed and debated every single year. In fact, it is the topic of the keynote address of the president at least every other year. So what is this science-practice gap, and why are we so concerned with it? This "gap" refers to the lack of alignment between the I-O academic community and I-O practitioners. A 2009 survey of I-O psychologists suggested that the gap exists for several reasons:

- Practice underutilizes available science and research.
- Science undervalues innovations in practice.
- Science does not produce research findings that are relevant to practice.
- Practice does not provide sufficient opportunities to research relevant issues.[1]

This survey was specific to the I-O community, but it has relevance to a much broader issue in human resources. As HR professionals, a significant opportunity exists to build our processes and programs based on applied, scientific research. There is also an opportunity for researchers to conduct more meaningful, practitioner-oriented research. In response to these existing needs, the purpose of this book is threefold:

- To summarize relevant applied research for key HR processes
- To describe best practices for each HR process
- To identify how to make the processes business-focused — link the processes to relevant business outcomes (i.e., show ROI for each process)

This book is written to assist HR practitioners in utilizing key research findings and best practices to design and implement more effective HR processes. Taking the key points from tested, reliable, valid, and objective research and incorporating them into the initiatives will improve execution, limit legal risks, keep human resources on the cutting edge, and most importantly, help human resources demonstrate business impact and return on investment (ROI).The goal is not to get hung up on the science or the math of the research; we are in the people side of the business — and that is a good thing. One of the goals of this book is to briefly summarize the scientific research for key HR processes to make human resources relevant, practical, and people-focused. Most HR practitioners understand why this goal is necessary, but just in case you are not convinced yet, we will review a simple example of this gap and the relevance of this book.

Let us consider employee selection, which is probably the most researched HR process of all. When it comes to selection, we know a lot about what works and what does not. The validity of the employee interview has been studied literally hundreds of times — probably more, but we could not finish the book if we counted all of them. The research shows that an unstructured interview is only slightly better than "chance" at selecting a high performer. This means that when hiring managers interview candidates in the typical "tell me about yourself" approach, the decision they make about whether or not to hire the candidates is only slightly better than flipping a coin. However, as HR practitioners, we also know that this method is exactly how most hiring decisions are made. Often an organization will have multiple people conduct an unstructured interview with a job candidate. This practice does not add any validity to the process — it just adds to the number of people flipping coins. Of course, ask hiring managers about their ability to make good hiring decisions, and they will respond with a resounding, "I am a great assessor of talent!"However, applied research suggests that the typical manager is *not* a great assessor of talent. Moreover, the unstructured interview process lacks legal defensibility and thus opens the door to lawsuits.

Applied research indicates that structured interviews (for example, behaviorally based interviews) are three or four times more valid than unstructured interviews. Knowing this simple fact makes it hard to stand behind unstructured interviewing. By simply defining the critical competencies (i.e., knowledge, skills, abilities, and behaviors) required to perform a role and then systematically assessing those competencies in a structured interview, HR practitioners can dramatically improve the hiring process for their organization. Of course, the trick is to develop structured interview processes that are simple and easy to use. We will tackle that topic further in Chapter 2. The point is that we know unstructured interview processes do not work well — from both research evidence and practical evidence. However, in many organizations they are the prevailing selection methodology applied for most jobs.

This book will provide the best practice for 11 critical HR processes, including employee selection. You will learn how to get the most out of an HR process, how to execute it properly, and how to determine the impact that it has had on business outcomes. All of this is accomplished by briefly examining applied research, incorporating practical experiences, and using analytics rather than depending on subjective, intuitive decisions.

As we reviewed the research that is available to practitioners to guide them in their practice, we found good material on bringing applied science to HR management.[2] However, we could not find a comprehensive resource that would help HR practitioners incorporate the best applied research in a pragmatic manner and show them how to make the direct connection between what they do every day and business outcomes. We found entire books (hundreds of pages) on multi-rater assessments, but the information was primarily presented in an abstract, theoretically oriented way, making it less relevant to the needs and interests of practically focused readers. Additionally, the sheer amount of information was overwhelming, thus getting in the way of its usefulness for practitioners with demanding day jobs. We found "best practice" documents that summarized the latest thinking about various HR processes. However, they were based solely on what "leading" organizations were doing regarding a specific issue or HR process. These best practices were not always based on research or ROI; they simply described the latest trends. Some of those untested trends in the last 20 years include quality circles, leaderless teams, and employee engagement — just a few consultant-driven trends that have no real definition and have rarely, if ever, shown a true impact on the business.

We decided to fill this science-practice gap with a practical book that summarizes the volumes of research for key HR processes and topics and describes it in a constructive manner that would lead to proven HR practices in the field. Quite frankly, we got tired of seeing organizations putting themselves at legal risk with their practices, not effectively executing initiatives, or not following through to show any business impact. All the while, volumes of applied research are available to guide organizations in their practices but no realistic and practical way to access and apply the information in business.

The Business Partner Roadmap

In our previous book, *Investing in What Matters*, we introduced the Business Partner RoadMap™. This proven process was outlined to help organizations discover and quantify the people drivers of business outcomes. Ultimately, this process allows organizations to create an HR strategy that is based on analytics, demonstrated business impact, and ROI.

As stated earlier, a primary goal of this book is to describe how to link core HR processes to relevant business outcomes (that is, show an ROI for each process).

Therefore, the application of the Business Partner RoadMap™ is relevant for our current purposes. So before we dive into the core HR processes, a brief review of the Business Partner RoadMap™ is necessary.

What Are the Steps For Linking Employee Data to Business Outcomes?

The Business Partner RoadMap™ is a six-step process (see Figure 1.1) that can drive your HR strategy by connecting what you do as an HR leader directly to the business.[3] It moves beyond conducting just analysis and creates an environment of executive buy-in, cross-functional interaction, targeted initiative building, and a culture of measurement and refocusing.

Figure 1.1 The Business Partner RoadMap™

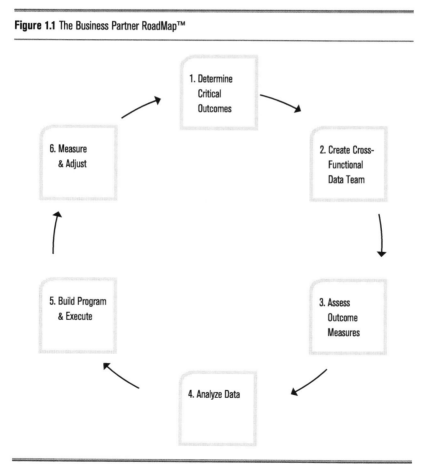

1. Determine Critical Outcomes

2. Create Cross-Functional Data Team

3. Assess Outcome Measures

4. Analyze Data

5. Build Program & Execute

6. Measure & Adjust

Step 1: Determine Critical Outcomes

An organization must first determine the top two to three most critical priorities that it anticipates will be accomplished through its employees. For example, increasing productivity or customer satisfaction and decreasing turnover are commonly desired outcomes. The outcomes that matter most to your organization can be gleaned by reviewing strategic documents and plans. Key stakeholder interviews of the board, CEO, CFO, or other business leaders are also very helpful in the process. Once this information has been collected and summarized, the results must be prioritized into two to three desired outcomes.

Step 2: Create a Cross-Functional Data Team

Once the various owners of the critical business metrics have been identified, a cross-functional data team (CFDT) needs to be organized. This team should consist of measurement experts, the key line of business leaders or metric owners, and HR leadership. The measurement experts are needed in order to determine data requirements, link the necessary datasets scientifically, and conduct the requisite statistical analyses. This cross-functional team will also facilitate and sponsor the linkage initiative. Therefore, having influential company leaders and decision-makers participate in this process is crucial. Often times, the data needed to build an HR strategy already exist. The key focus should then be pulling the data into one place to facilitate proper analysis.

Step 3: Assess Measures of Critical Outcomes

Once the critical outcomes have been identified, the next step is to determine how data are currently captured in the organization. Several characteristics of each outcome measure must be assessed, including the following:

- Frequency of measurement (e.g., monthly, quarterly, annually)
- Level of measurement (e.g., by line of business, by work unit, at the store level, at the organization level)
- Organizational owners of each of the outcome measures (e.g., the department or leader of the particular measurement)

It is critical to understand each of these measurement characteristics before any linkages to employee data can be made. The goal is to have apples-to-apples comparisons of the data.

Step 4: Objectively Analyze Key Data

This part of the process will require advanced statistical knowledge. Most large organizations employ statisticians or social scientists. If this type of internal resource does not exist in your organization, then hiring a consultant or full-time statistician for this role is necessary. This critical step is where the carefully collected datasets are statistically linked through various methodologies. Many business leaders are familiar with correlation and regression but not with a technique called structural equation modeling. Correlation is not sufficient, and regression is merely adequate. Structural equation modeling is the preferred solution for these types of data linkage analyses, as it accounts for measurement error, and cause-effect relationships can be inferred. Structural equation modeling affords us the ability to state, for example, that employees' attitudes about work/life flexibility are a cause-and-effect driver of increased customer satisfaction. This implied cause-effect relationship is important for understanding how these different measures relate to each other as well as for calculating an expected return on investment for the initiatives.

The statistical component of this step sounds complicated, but it is really just a tool for accomplishing three things:

■ Understanding the relationship between employee initiatives, skills, behaviors, attitudes, and meaningful business outcomes
■ Prioritizing types of interventions
■ Calculating expected ROI

All of this work is designed to allow you to identify organizational priorities and to determine appropriate levels of investment. The result of the data analyses is a list of key priorities, derived from the employee data that will drive the desired business outcomes. For example, the analyses may indicate that improving employee attitudes about work/life balance initiatives leads to increased employee productivity and customer satisfaction and decreased turnover. The results will also show which initiatives are not having their desired impact(s) and could be candidates for "cost cutting."

Step 5: Build the Program and Execute

Once the critical priorities have been identified, the next step is to determine what types of interventions will have the desired effect. This is the action-planning stage where activities can be focused at the systemic (organization-wide) level, line-of-business level, or work-unit level. This stage encompasses the bulk of the work and investment associated with any people-related process. The big difference is that the investments being made are focused on those employee processes, skills, attitudes, demographics, and other characteristics that have been shown to have a direct impact on the organization's desired business outcomes. The expected return can thus be used to guide the HR strategy.

A common trap at this stage is to look for the "silver bullet" of interventions. Best practices (another name for "silver bullets") are great to guide action planning. But simply replicating a "best practice" will get an organization nowhere. Initiatives must be customized and placed in the context of each unique organization. Throughout this book, we offer best practices as a guide to what has worked well at different points in time for other organizations. However, we caution readers against falling into the best-practice trap and blindly replicating these practices without considering what is most appropriate within the unique context of your organization.

Step 6: Measure and Adjust/Reprioritize

The last step is to re-measure in order to assess progress and calculate actual return on investment. Most business leaders understand the importance of goal setting and measurement. They also understand the importance of creating a culture of measurement and accountability. Similar to how other organizational decisions are made, slight adjustments to initiatives should be made along the way, based on regular measurement results. However, making frequent, wholesale changes to the strategic focus of the interventions is not advisable. In other words, pick your two to three priorities, and build action plans around those priorities. Measure progress against those plans two to three more times, and then recalculate the dataset linkages and reprioritize. This analysis process should occur annually. For your HR strategy, a yearly assessment of its overall effectiveness is in order, particularly when the annual budgeting cycle begins. Figure 1.2 outlines a high-level timeline of the analysis, strategy, and budgeting cycle.

Applying the Business Partner Roadmap to Core HR Processes

In addition to describing "best practice" and the practical application of applied research for each core HR process, we give practitioners the process and tools to transform HR procedures into business drivers as opposed to HR activities. For each HR process, we will discuss how to use the Business Partner RoadMap™ to connect the process to the bottom line. Each application will be highlighted by a case study to show you how the organizations we have worked with followed this process to customize their HR initiatives and make them business-focused.

Figure 1.2 The Annual Budgeting and Planning Cycle

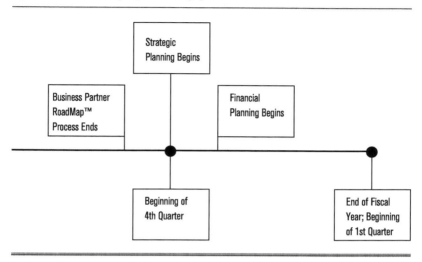

CHAPTER 2

Employee Selection

Most HR professionals understand the importance of making solid hiring decisions and the impact those decisions can have on the performance of the business. Although recruiting, assessing, and hiring the right people can be a time-consuming and challenging process, doing so pays off in terms of employee productivity, morale, and retention. Many organizations, both large and small, do not have disciplined or sophisticated approaches to the hiring process. Indeed, most continue to conduct unstructured interviews as their sole means of assessing job candidates. Despite many leaders' confidence in their hiring ability, their eye for talent is not as good as they might think.[1] As we discuss in this chapter, a structured selection process will help them make better hiring decisions. There are also several legal issues to consider when designing and implementing a selection system. We will not specifically address such issues, and we remind readers that the information provided in this chapter should not be considered legal advice.[2]

What the Research Tells Us

Effective Execution of a Structured Selection System

Research in the area of employee selection is quite robust and offers practical advice for HR professionals. We have outlined below the key steps to follow in designing and implementing a structured selection system for your organization.

Step 1: Conduct a Job/Competency Analysis

Prior to implementing a selection system, determine the knowledge, skills, abilities (KSAs), and competencies that job candidates need to have to be successful on the job. An analysis of the job itself will help those in the hiring position to accomplish the following:

- Understand the nature and purpose of the job.
- Identify any changes that are expected to affect the job tasks (e.g., technological advancements or structural changes).

■   Identify whether and how the KSAs will differentiate high performers from average performers.

■   Choose selection measures that are most relevant to job performance and are likely to yield the best selection decisions.[3]

(See Chapter 3 for additional details regarding the job analysis/competency modeling process.) Ultimately, having a comprehensive competency model or conducting a thorough job analysis for the key roles in your organization serves as the foundation for choosing appropriate selection tools and implementing an effective selection system.

Step 2: Choose the Appropriate Selection Tools

Employers may choose from a variety of selection tools. These tools are used after candidates' resumes have been screened and unqualified candidates have been removed from further consideration. The most commonly used tools include (1) pre-employment tests, (2) interviews, and (3) assessment centers.

Pre-employment tests.[4] Pre-employment tests are a straightforward approach to gathering information about job candidates that is relevant to the job and can be predictive of job performance. A variety of pre-employment tests may be used depending on the nature of the job and on the types of KSAs required of job candidates.[5] The most commonly used tests include:

■   *Personality tests.* Personality tests assess an individual's tendency to respond in a particular manner across a wide variety of situations. These tests are an excellent way of assessing whether a candidate is a good fit for a job. A number of personality traits have been found to predict future job performance. The most predictive trait is conscientiousness, a trait related to an individual's achievement orientation and dependability.[6] The specific traits to be assessed will vary depending on the job for which you are hiring and must be selected based on the results of the job analysis.[7]

■   *Cognitive ability tests.* Cognitive ability is the capacity to mentally process, comprehend, and manipulate information. It has consistently been found to be the best predictor of job training performance and technical job performance, particularly in highly complex jobs.[8] However, cognitive ability tests have been shown to have the potential to impact protected groups adversely.[9] As a result, these tests should not be the sole tool used to make hiring decisions.[10] Moreover, before using cognitive ability tests to select employees, organizations must prove that cognitive ability is a valid predictor of on-the-job performance.

- *Physical ability tests.* Physical ability tests are designed to assess a candidate's ability to perform physically demanding aspects of the job. These aspects may include lifting or pulling large amounts of weight or spending long periods of time sitting at a desk. Individuals who are physically qualified for the position are less likely to be hurt on the job.

When to use pre-employment tests. Pre-employment tests may be deployed at several points during the selection process:

- *During* the initial screening process to narrow the candidate pool prior to conducting interviews. A pre-employment test can be used as an initial screening assessment for a competency or skill that is deemed a "must-have" for a position — this definition often applies to physical ability tests. Candidates who do not meet the minimum requirements for the competency or skill can then be removed from the candidate pool.
- *After* the initial screening and interview to narrow the pool of candidates for a highly critical role. Well-validated pre-employment tests provide objective information that may be used to overcome subconscious biases and prejudices that can emerge in the interview process. The pre-employment test can thus be used to supplement information gained during the interview process and to help objectively distinguish qualified from unqualified job candidates.
- During the *initial* screening and *later* in the selection process. During the initial screening, candidates who do not meet the minimum requirements on a battery of pre-employment tests may be removed from the candidate pool. Those who do meet the minimum requirements may then continue with more costly application processes (for example, the interview or assessment center). Candidates' scores on the pre-employment tests may then be combined with their scores from other steps in the process and used to make a final hiring decision.

Interviews. Interviews are one of the most common and powerful job selection tools used by organizations today, as they provide an opportunity for the hiring manager and other stakeholders to get a first-hand glimpse of the job candidate's skills, abilities, and interpersonal style. There are two broad categories of selection interviews: unstructured and structured.

As the name implies, unstructured interviews are less structured and systematic. During unstructured interviews, candidates and interviewers discuss whatever topics the interviewers wish to explore. Interviewers are provided few guidelines with regard to the content of the questions or the format, and they may choose to ask different questions of each candidate. While there may be some consistency in the content and process of unstructured interviews for a given position, they are generally characterized by a lack of standardization across job candidates.

In contrast, structured interviews are standardized processes that are identical (or nearly identical) across all job candidates. The questions asked during the structured interview are designed to tap into various job-relevant dimensions, and the candidate's responses are evaluated by trained interviewers using a structured rating scale. Standard interview questions and rating scales help to enhance the validity of the structured interview, making it easier for interviewers to score candidate responses and draw comparisons across candidates. Over 100 years of academic and applied research has shown structured interviews to provide a more valid assessment of job candidates and to result in better hiring decisions.

Developing a structured interview guide. The main objective when writing interview questions is to cover only job-relevant information and to adequately address all salient job dimensions. Your structured interview guide should include the following essential types of questions:

- Tell me about a time when you… (asking for an event that may give evidence of a particular competency).
- In what key places in the event were you involved? At each point of involvement,
  - » What did you do?
  - » How did you do it?
  - » What were you thinking when you did that?
  - » What did you say?
  - » What was the outcome?

You should also avoid a few types of interview questions:

- Leading questions that suggest what the candidate should talk about or that hint at a particular answer (for example, Did you do any planning for that presentation? Were you feeling challenged?)
- Questions beginning with *Why*. These questions elicit present thoughts and rationalizations instead of revealing what a candidate thought in a past situation.
- Questions that can be answered "yes" or "no" (for example, Did you follow specific guidelines in preparing your presentation?)
- Questions that ask for opinions and attitudes (for example, What does leadership mean to you?)
- Judgmental questions that put people on the defensive (for example, Was that the best way to start that project?)
- Tangential questions that are unrelated to the focal job dimensions (for example, You just mentioned that you ride horses. What kind of horse do you ride?)

To standardize the scoring of interview responses, behaviorally anchored ratings scales (BARS) should be developed for each question. These scales help to standardize interviewer ratings across candidates and to focus interviewer attention on the most important aspects of the interview responses.

Here is an example of a competency with structured interview questions and follow-up probing items:

Competency: Financial Risk Assessment and Management

Recommended behavioral interview questions:

■ Tell me about a time when you established specific risk profiles and recommended tolerances, prioritized risks, and/or proposed changes in risk control investment.

■ Give me an example of a time when you successfully mitigated a significant risk for the organization.

Follow-up probes:

■ How did you develop the risk profiles?

■ What was the first step you took in mitigating this risk?

■ What was the outcome of the situation?

The BARS that the interviewer would use to effectively rate the candidate's answers to the structured interview items are depicted in Table 2.1.

Implementing a structured interview. Prior to implementing a structured interview, the interviewers (i.e., the raters) should be trained in the interview process. Ideally, the same set of interviewers will interview each candidate for a particular job. Interviewers need to rate each of the candidates' responses immediately after the interview question is asked to help prevent global impressions from biasing their rating and to ensure the most accurate assessment of each job dimension. Finally, the interviewers' ratings should be integrated with other components of the selection process to make the final selection decision.

Assessment centers. Assessment centers are a collection of activities designed to gauge the competence and qualifications of an individual for a given job. Although one of the most costly selection tools, well-designed assessment centers have been found to effectively differentiate between high- and low-performing candidates and to predict job performance and salary progression. Assessment center exercises provide hiring managers with unique opportunities to have job candidates demonstrate their skills in a variety of job-relevant areas (e.g., problem-solving, decision-making, influencing others, organizing and planning, communicating, and more). When implemented correctly, assessment centers can enhance selection validity, resulting in better selection decisions than when using pre-employment tests alone.[11]

Table 2.1

1. Proficiency	2. Strength	3. Mastery
■ Demonstrates understanding of the environment in which the organization operates, the strategic and financial objectives, and factors critical to success and identifies threats (and opportunities) related to the achievement of the objectives ■ Works with external resources to identify financial and operating risks and communicates them to senior management ■ Conducts risk analysis to determine potential opportunities and/or exposures ■ Provides input into the design of internal controls by providing insights on how to identify and measure risk areas ensuring the costs and benefits are properly analyzed ■ Assesses or oversees the assessment of risk (scope, nature, significance, and probability) and communicates these risks to senior management ■ Demonstrates understanding in the laws relating to foundations	■ Effectively communicates risks to gain organizational alignment for appropriate solutions ■ Trains others on linking macro-level risks (i.e. capital, internal controls) to financial performance in order to properly determine impact of potential risk areas ■ Establishes specific risk profiles and recommends tolerances, prioritizes risks, and recommends increase/decrease or change in risk control investment ■ Performs risk assessments for organizational area or entire network ■ Builds a "risk aware" culture within the organization ■ Provides appropriate training/education related to risk management ■ Ensures the board and staff know and adhere to all relevant state and federal laws and regulations ■ Ensures the budget complies with legal and fiduciary requirements ■ Assesses and manages and/or refers to legal counsel on potential conflicts with state and federal laws and regulations	■ Develops proactive and effective risk management programs, contemplating the cost and benefit of both the risk and the control activity undertaken ■ Manages and mitigates significant financial and operating risks to limit downside impact to the organization ■ Proactively influences organizational decisions/senior leadership by identifying strategies and tactics to mitigate macro level risk areas. ■ Drives sound organizational decisions by counseling senior management on risk management policy and strategies supportive of long-term operational and strategic objectives ■ Employs advanced risk management techniques such as risk transfer, risk financing, and risk avoidance to manage identified risks

Many possible choices for exercises to include in an assessment center exist, and the choice of which to use should be driven by the knowledge, skills/competencies, and abilities required on the job. Several of the most frequently used exercises are listed below:

- *Role playing/simulation*. Participants are given the chance to demonstrate their skills in a hypothetical work situation that closely resembles a situation they may encounter on the job. For example, candidates applying for a nurse position may have to demonstrate how they would handle a patient complaining about service in the hospital.
- *Leaderless group discussion*. This exercise is a popular way to assess leadership, teamwork, and communication style. Generally, a task is provided to a group of people with no assigned leader, and the group is expected to work toward a solution. The raters from the organization observe the level of involvement, leadership, teamwork, and other competencies to assess the qualifications and organizational fit of the candidates.
- *In-basket activities*. These exercises include a combination of several tasks such as a group of e-mails or descriptions of situations that are likely to be encountered on the job. For example, candidates may be asked to respond to e-mails from their manager, write a memo to their employees, or draft a press release to be distributed to external constituents.

When to use assessment centers. Assessment centers require a larger investment of time and money on behalf of the hiring organization than do many other selection tools. A number of direct costs are associated with developing and implementing the assessment center. In addition, indirect costs associated with the training of assessment center raters and the time spent by raters observing and evaluating assessment center performance also exist. Given the significant investment required to design and implement an assessment center, this selection tool is best used toward the end of the selection process when few candidates remain or for higher-level jobs. For most entry-level jobs, the costs of developing and implementing an assessment center are likely to be prohibitive. However, for jobs that are complex or supervisory in nature or that involve significant financial responsibilities, assessment centers are often a good choice. Assessment centers have the added benefit of being useful to determine promotions.

Step 3: Establish the Structure of the Selection Process

Ideally, the selection process will result in the hiring of a candidate or candidates who will achieve high levels of success on the job and in the rejection of those who would not be successful on the job. To maximize the hiring of the "right" person, decision-makers need to obtain a variety of job-relevant information using one or more of the tools discussed previously and to rely on statistical/mechanical models, rather than on their gut instincts, to make the final choice. In the absence of good procedures for final decision-making, employers are less likely to hire the best candidates and may inadvertently expose themselves to unnecessary legal risks.

Employers may choose from several selection system structures:

- *Multiple hurdle approach.* This structure involves establishing a chain of "hurdles" that a candidate must pass in order to move on to the next step in the selection process. For each hurdle, a minimum acceptable score (i.e., cut-off score) is established. Each selection test itself or aspects of each selection test (e.g., cognitive ability test, personality test, interview, or possession of a college degree) may be a hurdle. The most basic and must-have factors (such as education level or cognitive ability) are considered first and are used to quickly reduce the candidate pool. For example, an initial hurdle could be something as simple as the possession of a college degree. If candidates lack the degree, they are not considered for employment. This structure allows employers to refine the pool of job candidates without compromising the validity of the selection process.

- *Multiple cut-off approach.* This approach is similar to the multiple hurdle process in that for each predictor there is a minimum level or score that a prospective employee must meet in order to be considered for the job. However, instead of passing one hurdle at a time, as in the multiple hurdle approach, a candidate's scores on a variety of assessment tools are considered simultaneously. If the candidate scores high on a number of dimensions but does not achieve the cut-off score for one of the dimensions, he or she will be considered unfit for employment.

- *Compensatory approach.* This structure allows candidates to "make up" for a shortcoming in one critical area by possessing other positive qualities that offset the qualities they lack. Employers assign weights to each of the dimensions assessed during the selection process. These weights reflect the extent to which each dimension is relevant to job performance, with more heavily weighted dimensions being better predictors of performance. Using this structure, a high score on a heavily weighted job dimension can outweigh or help compensate for a low score on a lesser weighted dimension. In the compensatory approach, candidates are assessed on all relevant job dimensions and assigned weighted scores before the total score is calculated.

Depending on the specific needs and objectives of an organization, any of these selection structures could be appropriate. The main question that organizations need to answer is whether or not deficiencies in any dimension of job performance can reasonably be offset by other qualities. If so, a compensatory structure will be best. Additionally, organizations must consider whether or not they are willing to allow on-the-job training to compensate for weaknesses in candidates. While a candidate with all desired competencies would be ideal, sometimes on-the-job training is required to fill the gaps. Alternatively, if job candidates absolutely must possess one or more qualifications or skills (as is often the case in highly technical or specialized jobs), either a multiple hurdle or multiple cut-off approach tends to be most appropriate.

Step 4: Establish a Strategy for Making the Final Selection Decision

Once candidates' total scores have been calculated, the final step in the selection process is to make a hiring decision. If the selection system has been well-designed and appropriately implemented, the final pool of candidates will consist of job seekers who are highly qualified for the job. At this point, the goal is to select the top candidates (that is, those whose scores indicate they are likely to be effective in the job) while reducing bias to the greatest extent possible. Decision-makers can determine which candidates to reject and which to consider for employment using one of the following methods:

- *Cut-off score method.* The cut-off score method uses a selection ratio to determine which candidates to accept or reject. The number of open positions is divided by the number of expected candidates to compute the selection ratio, which tells how many candidates to accept and how many to reject. For example, if there are 10 open positions and 100 candidates, the ratio would be 10 percent ($10/100 = 0.10$ or 10 percent). If 90 percent of the candidates will be rejected, the cut-off score will be set at the 90th percentile of candidates' overall scores minus one standard error of measurement. According to the Equal Employment Opportunity Commission's (EEOC) *Uniform Guidelines*, the use of cut-off score selection is permitted when valid predictors (that are based on thorough and accurate job analysis data) are used.[12]

- *Top-down selection method.* Candidates' overall scores are rank-ordered from highest to lowest, and employment is offered to the candidates with the highest scores, continuing until all open positions are filled. If the job offer is declined by the top candidate, then an offer is extended to the next candidate on the list, and so on.

- *Banding.* Unlike the top-down selection method, the banding method assumes that scores within a specified range are equivalent. Candidates' scores are banded, or grouped, such that within each group differences in scores do not differentially predict on-the-job performance. As long as the candidates fall within the same band, their predicted job performance is assumed to be identical. For example, in a band ranging from 55 to 75, a candidate with a score of 60 is considered to be equivalent to a candidate with a score of 72. Candidates may then be randomly selected for hire from the top band.

While top-down methods offer simple solutions for final candidate selection, they can be problematic in some cases, particularly if cognitive ability tests are included in the model. There has been some research that suggests that, on average, black and Hispanic test-takers score lower on cognitive ability tests than do white test-takers.[13] Even in instances when cognitive ability is a valid predictor of job performance, if the results of these tests contribute too much to the final overall candidate score then using top-down selection procedures may result in adverse impact for minority candidates and possible EEOC violations. The same issue can be problematic when using cut-off scores.

Banding offers an advantage over top-down and cut-off score approaches in terms of possible biases, discrimination issues, and general legal defensibility. Banding candidates reduces the impact of measurement error; however, problems with adverse impact may arise if race or gender is used as the criterion for selecting candidates within a band. The best way to avoid legal pitfalls when using banding is to select candidates randomly from within each band instead of using criteria associated with protected group status (e.g., race or gender) to make your selection.

Building Business-Focused Selection Process

Hiring high-performing employees is one of the most valuable things you can do for your business. When the wrong person is hired for a job, the result is likely to be involuntary or voluntary turnover, costing the organization significant money, time, and energy. The specific costs associated with turnover vary by organization and job level but are commonly estimated at 100 percent to 150 percent of the base salary for the job. The stakes are even higher at the executive level. The direct costs associated with the loss of high-potential executives (i.e., separation, replacement, and training costs) have been estimated at two to three times the executive's salary. When indirect costs (such as the time and expenses associated with covering the vacancy and filling the vacant role) are factored in, the total can approach approximately four to five times the executive's salary.

Poor hires can also interfere with bottom-line organizational results, slowing production and inhibiting growth and innovation. As noted in a recent *HR Magazine* article, "When newly appointed leaders don't work out, valuable business knowledge can leave the organization — even to the competition — and the grueling recruiting process and costs start over again."[14]

More often than not, poor hiring decisions are the result of a poorly designed and/or (un)structured selection process. Although structured selection processes are more challenging to design and more time-consuming to carryout, their benefits to the business — in the form of reduced turnover and improved job performance — significantly outweigh any upfront investments in their development. Several metrics, including the return on investment (ROI), may be used to quantify the value of a structured selection system and enhance HR leaders' roles as strategic business partners. We will cover these metrics and demonstrate how to assess the ROI of your selection system in the following case study.

Case Study: Building the Business Case for Structured Selection Systems

As discussed above, researchers have consistently found structured selection processes to result in better hiring decisions than unstructured processes; the more structured the process, the better the hiring decisions. In the case study presented below, we demonstrate an effective approach to building the business case for a structured system in your organization.

We worked with a medium-sized pharmaceutical company looking to hire seventy new sales representatives. The first step in building the business case was to quantify for senior leaders the incremental validity of structured selection processes and the associated cost savings. In Table 2.2, we identify the number of poor hires (out of seventy) likely to result under a variety of different selection approaches.

The validity coefficients in the table indicate, based on years of research, how each selection approach compares to flipping a coin (50/50 chance of making a good hiring decision). With a validity coefficient of 0.10, unstructured interviews are only 10 percent more effective than flipping a coin, resulting in potentially 32 poor hires out of the 70 new hires. As evidenced in the table, the more sophistication and structure you add to the selection process, the lower your risk of making poor hiring decisions.[15]

Table 2.2

Approach	Validity Coefficient	Potential Number of Poor Hires
Unstructured Interviews	0.10	32/70
Behavior-based Structured Interviews	0.40	21/70
Multiple Hurdle Approach (e.g., Personality testing followed by a Structured Interview)	0.50	18/70
Assessment Center	0.60	14/70
Assessment Center – psychologists assessing candidates	0.70	11/70

Table 2.3 incorporates the assumption that the average cost of sales representative turnover is equal to the representative's annual salary of $50,000. Said otherwise, every poor hire costs the organization $50,000. The use of unstructured interviews alone in making hiring decisions is likely to cost the organization $160 million. Just by incorporating a behavior-based structured interview, we can reduce the number of poor hires by 11 and save the organization $550,000! These figures shocked senior-level decision-makers and readily convinced them of the need to invest in a structured selection process.

Table 2.3

Approach	Potential Number of Poor Hires	Expected Savings
Unstructured Interviews	32/70	
Behavior-based Structured Interviews	21/70	$550,000
BBI and Personality Assessment	18/70	$700,000
Assessment Center	14/70	$900,000
Assessment Center – psychologists assessing candidates	11/70	$1,050,000

Figure 2.1

Initial Phone Screen	Personality Inventory	Face-to-Face Interview	Role Play Scenario and Structured Interview
■ Delivered by recruiters	■ Conducted online by candidates	■ Structured, competency-based interview conducted by hiring managers	■ Role play, based on customer "meetings"
■ 30-minute screen to discuss fit, the role, job expectations, and provide a realistic preview	■ Provides overview of personality aspects and if candidate is a good fit for the role	■ Focused on specific behaviors and competencies required for the role	■ Structured interviews conducted by additional leaders
■ Candidates taken out or moved to the next step	■ **2nd Hurdle**	■ **3rd Hurdle**	■ Hiring managers trained on how to conduct/rate role plays
■ **1st Hurdle**			■ Comprehensive rating guides to assess performance
			■ **Final Hurdle**

Developing a Structured Selection Process

We conducted a thorough job/competency analysis to identify the critical knowledge, skills, abilities (KSAs), and competencies required for newly hired sales representatives to be successful. Based on the results of the job/competency analysis, we created the structured selection process depicted in Figure 2.1.

The use of multiple hurdles allowed us to save the organization money by eliminating unqualified candidates early in the process using more economical selection tools (that is, phone screens and the personality inventory) and by putting only the most qualified candidates through more costly and time-consuming portions of the process (the structured interview and assessment center).

On a project this large, it was critical that we keep a precise record of all job candidates and their performance at each step of the selection process, irrespective of whether they were ultimately hired. A proper and complete paper trail helps ensure the legal defensibility of your selection process, should any issues arise. The Selection Decision RoadMap™ depicted in Table 2.4 provides a straightforward way for hiring managers to document the performance of each job candidate and make appropriate hiring decisions. Using this RoadMap™, hiring managers were readily able to differentiate job candidates at every step of the multiple hurdle process and ultimately make objective, evidence-based hiring decisions.

Table 2.4 Selection Decision RoadMap™

Name	Phone Screen	Personality	Structured Interview	Role Play	Decision
Candidate #1	Highly Recommended	High Fit	4.8	4.6	Hire
Candidate #2	Highly Recommended	High Fit	4.0	4.3	Not Hire

Ensuring the Selection Process is Business-Focused

Contrary to popular practice, the selection process is not complete when all the positions have been filled. Instead, the KSAs and competencies used in the selection process as well as the components of the selection process itself should be constantly revalidated. By following the steps in our Business Partner RoadMap™, you can validate the selection process and demonstrate its impact on critical business outcomes.

The key questions to ask at each step of the Business Partner RoadMap™ are as follows:

1. *Determine critical outcomes.* What are the key outcomes/metrics for which the employees who went through the hiring process are now held accountable?

2. *Create a cross-functional data team.* Who owns the specific outcomes/metrics for these employees?

3. *Assess outcome measures.* Are the meaningful business data/metrics collected at the appropriate level — in this case, at the individual level?

4. *Analyze the data.* Did the pre-employment tests and assessment center exercises predict job performance (i.e., did higher scores during the hiring process lead to better job performance)?

5. Based on the analysis, what hiring process components are more or less valuable than others? Is a specific component underperforming? Should we enhance, eliminate, or change that component?

6. *Measure and adjust.* How do we ensure that the quality of our future hires remains high?

By demonstrating the connection between the selection process and new hire performance, this follow-up analysis helps reinforce the value of the structured selection process. Additionally, providing such data to senior leaders and skeptical frontline managers helps garner buy-in and ensure that the standardized processes are followed when making future selection decisions. Finally, this process allows HR leaders to demonstrate a return on investment (ROI), thus enhancing their role as strategic business partners. The ROI is calculated by aligning the selection assessment scores with the hired employees' job performance ratings/productivity numbers and other values. Using the methodologies discussed previously (i.e., structural equation modeling; see Chapter 1 for more information), you can definitively show that the structured hiring process, which consisted of an assessment of candidates' competencies, personality, experiences, and other characteristics resulted in high levels of on-the-job performance.

Practical Tips

The following recommendations will help you to implement a well-structured, business-focused selection system that enhances the quality of your hiring decisions and contributes to bottom-line organizational outcomes.

- Define performance criteria for each target position using a thorough job analysis or competency modeling approach.
- Choose specific selection tools based on these criteria:
  - » Level of the position
  - » Scope of performance criteria
  - » Budget for selection process
  - » Selection timeline

- » Size and demographics of the candidate pool
- » Concerns for candidate reactions
- Deliver necessary training to key staff involved in the selection process.
- Develop strategies for scoring and making final decisions prior to evaluating any job candidates. This step includes the following:
  - » How scores will be combined or weighted
  - » How final decisions will be made
  - » Who will make final decisions
- Systematically assess candidates and document their scores at every step of the selection process.
- Demonstrate the linkage between the selection tools/process and critical business outcomes (e.g., turnover or new-hire performance).

CHAPTER 3

Competency Models

Competency models have become increasingly popular in organizations over the past two decades, as they can provide a strong foundation for employee performance appraisals, leadership training and development initiatives, and promotion and succession decisions. Although competency models are quite widely used in organizational settings, research into the effectiveness of such models is sorely lagging behind. In this chapter, we draw upon the limited existing research to define competencies/competency modeling, offer evidence-based approaches on how to create and execute a strong competency modeling process, and discuss how to make your competency models focused on the business.

What the Research Tells Us

Competencies are broadly defined as sets of skills or abilities that are associated with effective job performance and/or leadership. More specifically, researchers have defined competencies as sets of behaviors instrumental in the delivery of desired results or as "observable, behavioral capabilities that are important for performing key responsibilities of a role or job."[1] Some researchers have expanded this definition, noting that competencies involve a generic body of knowledge, motives, traits, self-images, social roles, and skills that have a relationship to superior or effective performance on the job. Although a consistent definition of competencies is beginning to emerge, researchers and HR leaders continue to struggle to identify an agreed-upon approach to competency modeling.[2] Instead, approaches to competency modeling typically fall within three broad categories — educational, psychological, and business.[3]

The educational approach draws a connection between competencies and credentials. According to this approach, the accumulation of skills and the achievement of standards can be used to demonstrate an individual's "competence." For example, numerous educational degrees or certifications (for example, Ph.D. and SPHR) would be examples of educational competence.

The business approach tends to generalize individual or job-specific competencies to broader organizational-level competencies. Under this approach, competencies tend to be geared toward the achievement of organizational goals or strategies. An example would be the number of functions that individuals have performed and the results that they have achieved in those roles.

Finally, the psychological approach defines competencies as sets of motives and personality traits, most closely resembling the knowledge, skills, and abilities approach with which most HR professionals and other business leaders are familiar. For example, teamwork, mission-focus, planning, and influencing are just some of the numerous competencies that are articulated via competency models in organizations. This approach has been most widely adopted by researchers and practitioners and has some predictive value in terms of future workplace behavior and job performance.[4] We will show you how to assess the link between competencies and performance later in this chapter.

Competency Models versus Job Analysis

The similarity between competencies and the knowledge, skills, abilities, and other characteristics (KSAOs) traditionally assessed with a job analysis has created some confusion among researchers and practitioners. Competency models provide descriptions of sets of individual-level skills and abilities that are common among an occupational group or job level. Competencies tend to be more broadly applicable and leverage common or universal themes. Additionally, they are focused on *how* the work gets done rather than on *what* work gets done. As a result, competencies serve as an excellent guidepost for training and development initiatives designed to enhance broad sets of an employee's skills and abilities. In contrast, KSAOs tend to accentuate differences across jobs or occupational groups. Thorough job analyses are used to identify KSAOs that are highly job-specific or that predict performance in a narrow range of jobs or job types. Unfortunately, as we discuss below, the differences between competencies and KSAOs are often overlooked in practice, and the former have begun to serve as the foundation for a much wider array of HR practices (for example, hiring, promotion, and succession planning) than originally intended.

Researchers have struggled with the complexities and the validity of competency models for years. Researchers frequently ask the following questions:

- Are competencies credible in organizations?
- Can competencies be measured accurately?
- How can organizations account for extra-role or organizational citizenship behaviors within a competency framework?

- With the constant shifting of job responsibilities and the open-ended job description, what is the shelf life of a competency model?
- Do improved competencies predict improved individual job performance and/or improved organizational performance?

Effective Design and Execution

Competency models generally consist of 8 to 16 competencies that are clustered by type (for example, task management, people management, and communication). Each competency is labeled and clearly defined, as well as anchored by several example behaviors that distinguish the competency. Examples of commonly used competencies that reflect the work performance domain include leading/deciphering, supporting/cooperating, interacting/presenting, analyzing/interpreting, creating/conceptualizing, organizing/executing, adapting/coping, and enterprising/performing. These competencies, or variations thereof, are repeated in organizational competency models across a wide range of organizational types and industries. Such models are intended to serve as a blueprint for outstanding performance, helping employees to identify the skills and abilities that are valued by the organization and that foster advancement and long-term success. Competency models are often viewed as a roadmap of behaviors that can be used to recruit, attract, retain, reward, compensate, and develop employees while adding strategic advantage to the organization.

The actual process of creating competency models involves identifying and defining the competencies, or combinations of knowledge, skills, traits, and abilities, that enable effective job performance or leadership within the context of a particular organization.[5] There are several possible ways of developing an organizational competency model, such as utilizing do-it-yourself processes that rely heavily on generic competency dictionaries,[6] selecting an off-the-shelf competency model,[7] or employing consultants to develop a customized model. As you might imagine, the do-it-yourself and off-the-shelf approaches, although attractive, may not be specific enough to your organization and culture to have a meaningful impact. Additionally, off-the-shelf approaches rarely receive a high level of buy-in from senior leaders and front-line managers.

In contrast, developing a customized competency model, with or without the assistance of consultants, ensures that the competencies selected for inclusion in the model are aligned with the organization's values and performance expectations and helps facilitate buy-in from senior leaders early in the competency modeling process. Although a comprehensive, research-based approach to competency modeling has yet to be developed,[8] the following have been identified as critical steps in the competency modeling process:

- Use existing job-relevant materials (e.g., job descriptions) and organizational directives (e.g., mission or strategic objectives) to inform the selection of appropriate competencies.
- Work closely with senior managers in the development of the competency model to ensure that you have their buy-in and support.
- Demonstrate the link between competencies and business outcomes.
- Implement the new competency model in phases to solicit buy-in across the organization.
- Integrate with existing training/development and performance management practices.
- Reevaluate your competency model on a regular basis to ensure that the competencies are still relevant to individuals and jobs across the organization.

Building Business-Focused Competency Models

To have the greatest impact, your competency modeling efforts must be aligned with relevant business outcomes. In this section, we outline the steps you can take to make the competency modeling process business-focused from start to finish.

1. *Collect data from multiple perspectives.* Too often HR leaders and consultants rely solely on interviews with current employees/incumbents (i.e., those currently holding the job or role of interest) as the cornerstone of their competency modeling process. This strategy is shortsighted and does not provide the depth of information needed to identify the critical competencies for particular jobs or roles. Collecting data from incumbents, leaders, and internal or external customers, using multiple formats (interviews, surveys, sorting exercises), will help maximize the depth of information obtained and enhance the relevance of the resulting competency model.

2. *Integrate the data from multiple perspectives.* Just having data from multiple perspectives is not enough. The data must be analyzed separately and then brought together to tell a cohesive story around the critical KSAOs along with "how" the job needs to get done — to create a strong competency model.

3. *Focus on a specific goal or a set of goals.* Doing so reinforces the alignment between the competency modeling process and other organizational needs and helps create a sense of urgency. The case study that follows starts with selection and development as the key goals.

4. *Use a sorting exercise with key stakeholders.* Once you have collected your KSAOs from the multiple data points, gathering key subject matter experts

and other knowledgeable stakeholders for a "sorting" exercise is advisable. During this facilitated exercise, they will be asked to sort the detailed KSAOs into the broader competency buckets and come to consensus on their decisions as a group. This exercise will increase buy-in for the process and enhance the relevance of the resulting competency model.

5. *Make the process practical.* Technical jargon and fancy acronyms do not impress senior or front-line leaders. When describing the competencies needed for particular roles, use readily understandable terms such as "must-have," "needed to win," and "differentiator." This is not "dumbing it down"; this is making a somewhat tedious process interesting and bringing it to a level where action can be taken.

6. *Establish a buy or build strategy.* When using a competency model for selection needs, key stakeholders should decide whether to hire external candidates who possess the desired competencies (i.e., buy) or to provide internal staff with training on the competencies (i.e., build). Careful assessments of time, effort, and budget will play a big role in this decision.

7. *Set minimum requirements.* Once the competencies have been selected, minimum acceptable levels of performance on each of the competencies must be defined. Specifically, HR leaders and managers across the organization must understand the minimum level at which individuals can perform and still be successful in their roles.

8. *Link to business outcomes.* This step is straightforward if you follow the Business Partner Roadmap™ — discover the key business outcomes; assess the competencies (for example, during selection or performance appraisal processes); line up the competency data and business outcome data; and analyze using structural equation modeling. This process will "validate" the competency model and also show its direct business impact. Additionally, this procedure will solidify buy-in from senior leaders and front-line managers and will help drive your training, hiring, and performance appraisal strategies because you will know what competencies to focus on based on their importance to the bottom line.

9. *Continue to refine the model and the strategy around it.* The roles for which you built the competency model may change over time, so revisiting the model every 18 months to ensure its comprehensiveness and relevance is recommended. At the same time, reexamining the buy/build strategy that was created for the particular role is beneficial. For example, the training for a competency may have been brought in-house, or the budget may allow for a vendor — these options can create an opportunity to build the necessary skills versus buying.

10. *Include standards of performance.* Many organizations place a strong focus on their mission, vision, and values, but far fewer make the values, or standards of performance, a central part of their competency model. Standards represent a key piece of *how* the job gets done. When appropriate, incorporate your standards into the mix.

11. *Generic models are not enough.* Broad, all-encompassing competency models are faster to put down on paper — but that is it. They do not provide any real value in terms of driving accountability or building training, selection, or performance appraisal strategies. To make your competency model more specific, consider including *foundational competencies* that are applicable to all roles, *strategic competencies* that are pertinent to specific roles (e.g., leaders), and *functional competencies* that are specific to particular functions or departments.

Case Study: Building a Competency Model for a New Role

A midsize pharmaceutical company was in the process of launching a new product that was very different from its core product line. The product launch created challenges on many fronts, especially for the sales organization and human resources. In particular, the organization recognized the need to build a new sales force competency model that better captured the competencies necessary to be effective in managing the types of accounts associated with the new product. The specific goals of this competency modeling initiative were as follows:

- To objectively identify the skills necessary to excel at managing the new types of accounts
- To develop a comprehensive competency model and job descriptions for the new sales force
- To identify, for each competency, an overall buy versus build strategy for the sales force
- To provide input into the training/development and performance management strategies used with the sales force

We followed the 11 steps outlined above to help the organization create a business-focused competency model that leaders at all levels supported.

Our specific approach follows.

Conduct Stakeholder Interviews

The stakeholders included senior sales leaders, front-line sales managers, sales representatives currently working in the organization, outside sales experts, and doctors/prescribers working within the specialty. The focus of the interviews was to discover (1) the KSAOs of the sales role and (2) the unique KSAOs of selling this very different type of product in the market.

Survey Multiple Stakeholder Groups

Once the interviews were completed, the feedback on the KSAOs was integrated into a more manageable list of behavioral statements (for example, "secures commitment to prescribe"). We then created three separate surveys for the key stakeholder groups. First, we surveyed (online) a nationwide group of doctors who work in the specialty area. The goal was to gain quantitative insight into the qualities and services that define best-in-class sales representatives who sell this specific type of product.

Second, we surveyed (by phone) a group of high-performing sales representatives from outside the organization who have sold this type of product in the past. The goals here were to gain (1) quantitative insight into the skills and behaviors that drive success in selling this type of product from a sales-representative point of view and (2) qualitative insights by obtaining open text input into key behaviors and skills that drive successful selling of this type of product.

The third survey conducted was with senior leaders at the client organization. This survey focused on the behavioral statements obtained during the stakeholder interviews. We asked leaders to rate the level of importance of each of the behavioral statements, which allowed us to prioritize each of the KSAOs.

Integrate and Present Data to Decision-Makers

The goal of this step was to get all the decision-makers on the same page by presenting them with the comprehensive data collected during the interviews and integrating it into a cohesive story about the link between KSAOs and sales representative performance. By feeding this information to senior decision-makers in a straightforward (and relatively brief) presentation, we were able to show them the data-driven prioritization of KSAOs, which we categorized as Must-Have, Needed-to-Win, and Differentiator. This step provided the foundation to move onto the next phase, which was sorting the KSAOs into key competencies.

The Competency Sorting Exercise

Based on all the data we collected from multiple stakeholders, a framework of seven broad competencies had begun to emerge. To make the sorting exercise a starting point, we shared these competencies and asked stakeholders to sort the KSAOs into the competency "buckets." The stakeholders worked as a group to discuss each KSAO and place it into the appropriate competency bucket. However, the competencies that we started with were not written in stone; if a KSAO did not seem to fit into any of the original competency "buckets," then a discussion was held about creating a new competency or expanding the scope of a current one. The sorting exercise was complete when the stakeholders reached a consensus on the final set of competencies and corresponding KSAOs.

Final Prioritization of Competencies

Once the final competencies had been agreed upon, the level of importance for each one was calculated based on the importance of the KSAOs that made up each of the competency (as identified during the sorting exercise). Each competency was then classified as a Must-Have, Needed-to-Win, or Differentiator.

Buy versus Build Strategy

The prioritization of the competencies served as the foundation to help leaders think through whether to adopt a buy (hire off the street) or build (train internally) strategy for each of the competencies. Reaching consensus on the buy versus build strategy is critical for new jobs, as it will drive the development of the job descriptions for recruiting, hiring, and the training strategy for the organization. The buy versus build decisions should be driven by cost, time, and complexity considerations. Training leaders from the organization should be present for these discussions since they will understand the internal training capabilities for each of the competencies and will likely be affected by the buy/build decision. For this organization, leaders decided to "buy" depth of knowledge/experience in Medicaid and pharmaceutical regulations but to "build" the specific approach to selling (evidence-based selling). Training a sales person on all aspects of government regulations for the products would be extremely difficult and time intensive; however, the sales technique training could be administered, practiced, and mastered in a relatively short timeframe.

Minimum Requirements

The next step was to determine the minimum requirements needed for the role. Here we used the data from the high-performing sales representative phone surveys. The experience and knowledge level of the sales representatives were used as an initial proxy to make data-driven decisions about minimum requirements for the new role.

Armed with the information obtained from this process, job descriptions were created and the comprehensive hiring process — which assessed the sales representative candidates on all key competencies — was developed. The identification of minimum requirements also focused the organization on the critical areas in which immediate training was needed for the new sales representatives.

Linking Competencies to Business Outcomes

Approximately six to nine months after the hiring process was complete, we validated that the competencies created (and hired on) were driving business outcomes. The company focused on market share as the business outcome of interest. We lined up sales representatives' competency ratings from the hiring process (obtained during interviews and role plays) and their business performance ratings (market share was the organization's preferred metric). Using this data, we were able to show the level of impact of each competency on market share (using structural equation modeling and linkage analysis). This step helped prioritize each competency in terms of the level of market-share impact and validated the competency model by demonstrating that the level of performance on the competencies played a significant role in driving market share. This result solidified the use of competency models throughout the new sales force for hiring, appraisals, and development. A couple of the competencies were not highly predictive of business outcomes, giving us the opportunity to refine those specific competencies to make them more robust and relevant.

Ultimately, this organization produced a competency model that (1) was aligned to the business, (2) had senior- and front-line-level involvement, (3) was finalized by focusing on business needs and abilities (buy versus build), and (4) was a driving force of a critical business outcome (market share).

Some nuances to the process of building out a competency model for a new role exist. Let us turn our attention to a case study that describes a process for building competency models for existing roles within a large department.

Case Study: Competency Models as a Training Strategy Foundation

A large organization with a research and development function needed to build out a core set of competencies with the goal of creating a foundation for curriculum development. The vision for the function was to create a pipeline of products and people.

Although we cover building a training strategy in more detail in Chapter 7, reviewing the business-focused approach you can take is valuable. As usual, the business strategy needs to be the foundation of everything that HR leaders do. The next step is to define organizational capabilities (the organization's ability to manage its people to gain a competitive advantage) and identify the competencies that ultimately drive the business strategy — in this case a training/curricula strategy. Figure 3.1 shows the process in detail.

Figure 3.1

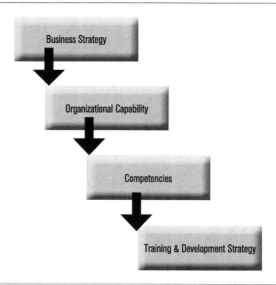

Organizational capabilities are higher-order factors that drive the entire organization to perform and are typically defined by senior leaders. Figure 3.2 shows examples of organizational capabilities as compared to competencies for a research and development function.

Figure 3.2

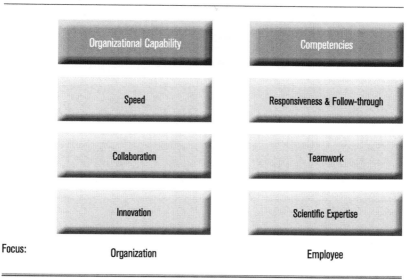

Organizational Capability	Competencies
Speed	Responsiveness & Follow-through
Collaboration	Teamwork
Innovation	Scientific Expertise

Focus: Organization   Employee

The organizational capabilities provide a foundation that can guide the strategy-building process, helping to ensure that the final strategy is linked to the organizational capabilities with the competencies as the execution conduit between the two.

In putting the entire process together, multiple levels of analysis for the research and development function should be present — starting with defining the organizational capabilities and then building out the specific competency models. Figure 3.3 represents the holistic process undertaken to accomplish the organization's three goals: (1) develop capabilities for the research and development (R&D) function, (2) create overarching R&D competency models for Leadership roles and Individual Contributor roles, and (3) create role-specific competency models for research executive, research manager, and research analyst.

Figure 3.3

Identify Capabilities for
the R&D Function

Create Two Distinct
R&D Competency
Models

Create Job Family
or Role Specific
Competency Models

Figure 3.4

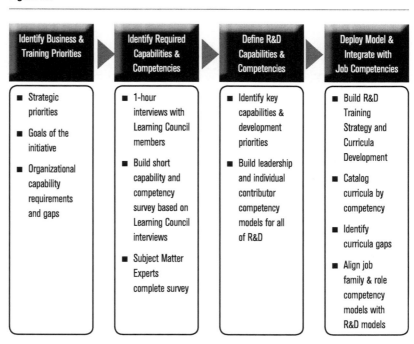

To build out the R&D competency models and the role-specific competency models, organizations have two primary options. The first, the top-down approach, depicted in Figure 3.4, is where the competency models are built by interviewing members of a learning committee (composed of subject-matter experts in training) and by surveying subject-matter experts in the various R&D roles. The competency models are built and then rolled out to the organization and become the foundation for the training curricula, which can be cataloged by competency in this particular case.

The second option, the bottom-up approach, involves developing an agreed-upon strategy for building the competency model(s) and then training internal resources within the R&D function, for example, to do the work (see Figure 3.5). The key to success when using this approach is to have a governance process in place to ensure alignment, consistency, and quality.

Figure 3.5

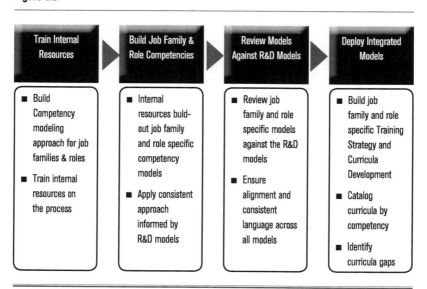

This particular organization used the bottom-up approach. The outcomes of this process yielded three strong competency models that were shown to drive performance outcomes (e.g. research production) in the R&D function. Two sample competency descriptions are listed in Table 3.1.

Table 3.1

Managing Research	Scientific Expertise
Changes research priorities when appropriate, based on input from management and available resources	Communicates own expertise to peers
Meets deadlines in spite of obstacles	Communicates own knowledge to others with different expertise
Ensures accuracy of research	Keeps up to date on scientific research
Matches tasks and appropriate resources to subordinate skill level	Publishes own research
Experiments with novel approaches in problem solving	Broadens expertise to respond to changing priorities
Applies a systematic approach to organizing research projects	Recognizes and exploits scientific opportunities
Understands research priorities and seeks appropriate resources to support them	Demonstrates the ability to effectively apply scientific techniques and knowledge

We used the same process outlined in the first case study to show the connection between the competencies in the competency model and the business outcome (research production). Specifically, competency data for each researcher was aligned with his or her research production numbers. The linkage analysis, which was conducted using structural equation modeling, allowed us to show the level of impact of each competency on research production.

In this case study, an existing role was the focus, but the key tenets were still the same. The goal of our competency modeling initiative was to gain insight from multiple perspectives on the competencies, align them to the business, and ultimately connect individual competencies to business outcomes. At the conclusion, each organization had a competency model that had strong buy-in across the board and that demonstrated links to critical business outcomes.

Practical Tips

- Involve stakeholders at the highest levels, both inside and outside human resources, to maximize buy-in for the process.
- Integrate the input you receive from multiple perspectives to create the most complete and comprehensive plan of attack to build the competency model.
- Gain a strong understanding of the role and the needs or limitations of the business to advise leaders on making buy versus build decisions on specific competencies for new roles.

- Define specific business-focused competencies for critical roles to maximize the effectiveness of the competency model for hiring, developing, and appraising performance.
- Collect data on competency ratings for current employees and applicants to use in the linkage analysis to show the impact of competencies on business outcomes.

CHAPTER 4

Performance Management

Performance management and appraisal are almost universally applied practices in organizations. Although they have evolved over the years, the key tenets of effective performance management have remained unchanged. However, the research and our own experience reveal several evidenced-based approaches that we have found to increase the impact of the performance management process in organizations. In addition, reliance on regular measurement and sophisticated analytical techniques can help make the process more business-focused. In this chapter, we will review all these key components of performance management.

What the Research Tells Us

The mechanics of the actual performance management appraisal tool have been extensively, if not exhaustively, researched for years. In the following section we review several key research findings and their implications for the practice of performance management.

Defining Performance

Researchers have struggled to reach a consensus on what constitutes job performance. Some have defined it as the behaviors aimed at achieving organizational and personal goals. This interpretation puts the focus on the behaviors of employees and not on the business outcomes resulting from those behaviors. John P. Campbell argued that the distinction between the goal-directed behaviors themselves and the effectiveness of those behaviors is critical because some outcomes of job performance are not fully under the control of the individual and therefore cannot be appropriately attributed to the employee.[1] For example, a salesperson engages in a number of behaviors, such as calling potential customers, building and maintaining relationships with new and existing customers, and troubleshooting customer questions and concerns. These behaviors are intended to produce the desired outcome of generating sales revenue. However, a number of factors besides the salesperson's behaviors, such as economic conditions, billing issues, or changes in customer preferences may influence the sales revenues that are generated.

Other researchers have defined job performance as the behaviors of employees and the way in which the outcomes of these behaviors contribute to the achievement of organizational goals.[2] This description encompasses both the behaviors themselves and the results of those behaviors. This definition connects well with the way performance management is conducted — with a focus on objectives and competencies — and is the definition of performance most frequently adopted by organizations.

Fairness

Once performance has been defined, the next step is to consider how the performance management and appraisal process itself will make employees feel. Performance management and appraisals can bring about feelings of unfairness because they are ratings of personal performance and compensation is typically involved. Researchers have found the following techniques to improve perceptions of fairness in the performance management process:

- Offering more frequent appraisals
- Engaging in joint goal planning between managers and employees
- Enhancing the manager's knowledge of what employees do in their roles

Rating Scales

Numerous rating scales used to make performance ratings are available. We will consider two well-validated approaches. Behaviorally anchored rating scales (BARS) focus on what a person might do in a given hypothetical situation with descriptions for high, medium, and low levels of performance.[3] An example is provided in Figure 4.1.

A potentially more relevant approach is behavioral observation scales (BOS), which requires the rater to rate employees on how frequently they have been observed by managers, peers, subordinates, and others acting in a particular way. For example, the statement "Goes above and beyond job duties to help teammates" would be rated on a five-point scale ranging from Almost Never to Almost Always.

Rating Distortions

Substantial research has investigated rating distortion in the performance appraisal process.[4] Although identifying the types of distortions that can occur (or have

Figure 4.1

Sample Behaviorally Anchored Rating Scale

QUALITY OF WORK, ACCURACY

How would you rate this individual with respect to the quality of the work he turns out, the neatness and accuracy evident in the job he does?

☐ Careless worker. Tends to repeat some types of errors.

☐ Work is sometimes unsatisfactory because of errors or untidiness.

☐ Usually turns out acceptable work. Not many errors.

☐ Checks and observes his work. Quality can be relied upon.

☐ Work is of highest quality. Errors extremely rare, if any. Little wasted effort.

COMMENTS: _____
_____

occurred) in your performance management system is meaningful, understanding how to fix the distortions is more advantageous. Unfortunately, researchers have not yet nailed down how to fix the problems. The key distortions are the following:

- *Central tendency error:* Raters use the midpoint to rate performance.
- *Leniency error:* Raters give ratings that are too high across the board.
- *Severity error:* Raters give ratings that are too low across the board.
- *Halo error:* Raters allow positive performance in one area to inflate ratings positively in other areas.

Being aware of these distortions is crucial for HR practitioners; however, a well-designed performance management system with clearly defined competencies and objective goals will reduce the problems that may arise from these distortions.

The research also suggests that employees should be included in the development and implementation of performance management processes and that the objective is not solely to improve employee performance; the goal is also to increase organizational innovation and maximize long-term organization growth.[5] Some have argued that performance management should be thought of as a partnership or dialogue between employees and their managers in which both parties are responsible for identifying and working toward specified goals. However, performance management can often be a one-way street in which the manager sets all the goals with little input from the employee. Indeed, performance management is often viewed as such in practice. Defined in this manner, employees become active participants in the management of their own performance and assume a portion of the responsibility for seeking performance feedback, coaching, and developmental opportunities. A number of practices, including the delivery of job-relevant feedback and learning and development opportunities, the identification of organizational career paths, and recognition and rewards for top performers, are often implemented to augment the basic goal-setting and performance appraisal process.

Effective Execution

Although specific practices vary, the basic performance management process has been well established and tends to be consistent across most organizations. The basic process allows managers to assess individual performance, optimize productivity, and ensure that employees' day-to-day actions are aligned with the organization's strategic goals. The best practices can be summarized in the following steps:

1. Establish the organizational strategy and ensure proper alignment between individual goals and the overall strategic objectives; cascade individual objectives and goals to employees or workgroups from corporate, division, and other sections.
2. Identify performance measurement parameters (performance expectations); clarify the accountability process; and measure competencies and results.
3. Provide ongoing coaching.
4. Tie the ratings to learning and development (more on this topic later).
5. Clearly differentiate performance ratings.
6. Differentiate high performers by giving them incentives (merit increases, long-term incentives).
7. Measure and document individual performance regularly.
8. Provide employees with ample job-relevant feedback.[6]

Setting and Aligning Goals

Baptist Health Care in Pensacola, Florida, is focused not only on setting goals at the organizational level but also on cascading those goals throughout all levels of leadership. The organization's highly effective process is as follows:

1. Senior team sets strategic organizational goals.
2. Goals are shared with all managers.
3. Managers draft departmental and individual goals and weights.
4. Goals and weights are confirmed with reporting supervisor.
5. Goals are aligned vertically and horizontally.
6. Goals are finalized through an alignment exercise and equity review.
7. Goals are openly communicated to staff and tied to behaviors.

The goals reported on every manager's performance plan follow the key aspects of the SMART acronym:

- S – Specific
- M – Measurable
- A – Action Oriented
- R – Realistic and Relevant
- T – Time Bound

As we mentioned earlier, it is essential to measure not only performance results (the "what") but also the behaviors/competencies/standards of performance required to obtain those results (the "how"). Figure 4.2 is an example of a performance plan from a leader at Baptist Health Care.

This approach captures all the key elements of a quality performance plan and is consistent with both research and practical recommendations.

Giving employees and managers a specific idea of what the actual evaluation process will look like is imperative. The steps in the actual evaluation phase typically include the following:

Figure 4.2

PEOPLE	SERVICE	QUALITY	FINANCE
Weight 20%	Weight 25%	Weight 15%	Weight 20%
Goal: Reduce annualized turnover to 15% with a stretch goal of 9% for fiscal year.	**Goal:** Achieve a percentile rank of 95 with stretch goal of 99 measured by vendor for nursing for the fiscal year.	**Goal:** Decrease pressure ulcers to less than 2 occurrences for last 6 months of fiscal year	**Goal:** Manage unit productivity to budget.
Metric: $\leq 9.0 = 5$ $12.0 - 9.2 = 4$ $15.0 - 13.0 = 3$ $20.5 - 15.1 = 2$ $\geq 20.6 = 1$	Metric: $\leq 99 = 5$ $97 - 98 = 4$ $95 - 96 = 3$ $90 - 94 = 2$ $\geq 89 = 1$	Metric: $\leq 0 = 5$ $1 - 1 = 4$ $2 - 2 = 3$ $3 - 3 = 2$ $\geq 4 = 1$	Metric: $\leq 105.0 = 5$ $103.0 - 104.9 = 4$ $100.0 - 102.9 = 3$ $90 - 94 = 2$ $\geq 89 = 1$

1. Standard of Performance: Ownership–**Sense of Ownership**
   Measurable Goal=Take responsibility for my team's actions by ensuring hand washing compliance is 100%
2. Standard of Performance: Attitude–**Commitment to Co-Worker**
   Measurable Goal=Link recognition and rewards to achieving performance excellence by submitting 100% of evaluations on time.
3. Standard of Performance: Customer Focus–**Customer Engagement**
   Measurable Goal=Listen to customers' concerns by round on 100% of my patients on my floor every day.
4. Standard of Performance: Customer Focus–**Responsiveness**
   Measurable Goal=Host monthly staff meetings to review HCAHPS and to communicate changes in policy, process, and important information.

1. *Self-evaluation.* Employees should complete a self-appraisal and provide it to the manager. The self-appraisal becomes part of the official appraisal. Gaps that may arise between the manager evaluation and the self-evaluation provide valuable coaching opportunities for managers and, if necessary, HR professionals to identify the reasons for the gaps.

2. *Manager-evaluation.* The manager sets up the appraisal meeting and prepares for it. Managers should complete their performance objectives and competency assessments of the employee beforehand and have the necessary paperwork available at the time of the meeting.

3. *Performance meeting.* The manager and employee discuss the appraisal. The discussion should focus on accountability to the performance goals and living up to the behaviors/standards within the organization. You might call this the "what" (task and goal achievement) and the "how" (the demonstrated behaviors/competencies of performance). This meeting is when the manager rewards the "what" and coaches to the "how." In addition, managers should do the following:

    a. State the agenda and purpose of the meeting.

    b. Review actual performance against each objective.

    c. Discuss the competency level/score for each competency.

    d. Discuss reasons for successes and, if necessary, challenges/problems/obstacles.

    e. Discuss the overall evaluation summary.

    f. Create a development plan.

    g. Finalize an overall rating.

Managers need to be fully aware that if the employee has earned negative ratings, then the employee's reactions will likely be negative. The SARA (Surprise, Anger, Resistance, and Acceptance) model will help managers and employees work through negative feedback more effectively (see Table 4.1). By recognizing this common emotional response to negative feedback, the manager/coach can anticipate the reaction and allow the employee to appropriately progress through the stages.

Table 4.1

Reaction	Description
Surprise	Surprised by unexpected feedback
Anger	Anger follows surprise; seen as a personal attack
Rationalization	Tendency to explain away the feedback
Acceptance	Realize that perceptions are reality

In addition, when delivering negative feedback, managers should consider their own safety and that of the staff. If managers know that the review will be particularly negative then they have some burden of responsibility to notify human resources and to potentially contact security.

Here are some additional suggestions you can communicate to help your employees process the feedback:

- The goal of providing feedback is to help employees improve their performance.
- We all have strengths and weaknesses — exceptional leaders understand both and work to improve weaknesses.
- This evaluation is an opportunity to learn more about yourself and become more self-aware.
- If you have questions while you are processing this feedback, ask me or someone else you trust for help or clarification.
- It is OK to disagree, but give yourself a couple of days to process the feedback before you reject it.

Organizations can take a number of approaches to enhance the effectiveness of their performance management process:

- *Clear communication.* When building and implementing a performance management strategy, clear and consistent communication is essential. Effective communication can help garner buy-in across organizational levels, clarify performance expectations, and align organizational strategies with employees' day-to-day actions.
- *Consistent delivery.* Performance evaluations and the delivery of incentives should take place in a clear and consistent manner. To be perceived as fair, performance evaluations must be as standardized as possible across employees. To this end, managers and employees should be trained in how to develop appropriate performance goals and use established performance metrics to evaluate employee performance. Additionally, incentives (for example, compensation) should clearly be connected to performance, and top performers should be recognized and rewarded.
- *Re-evaluate and update regularly.* To remain effective and relevant, the performance management process itself should be reevaluated and updated by the HR team (with the input of other key stakeholders) on an annual basis.

A concern about the performance management process is whether it should be used for administrative decisions or for developmental purposes. Many organizations attempt to combine the two purposes by using the performance appraisal to make administrative decisions (for example, to give bonuses or incentives) as well as to establish employees' career development goals. Holding effective conversations about the previous year's performance and about future opportunities in the same meeting is difficult for managers — especially if the review is not overly positive. An effective way to mitigate this issue is to conduct an annual performance review that is focused purely on reviewing the year's results and then have a separate, mid-year review to focus on the developmental opportunities for the employee.

A nonprofit organization, Feeding America, has incorporated this process as a way to tackle the administrative/developmental issue. The goals of its mid-year review are to accomplish the following tasks:

- Formally discuss career/skill development plans.
- Check in on the employee's annual goals:
  » Is the goal still relevant?
  » Does the goal need to be changed?
  » How is the employee performing against the goal?
- Provide feedback and coaching (which should also occur at regular intervals throughout the year).

The key tenets here are to take the evaluation piece out of the conversation and focus nearly all the discussion on development. We cover this process in depth in Chapter 8. Considering this approach is worthwhile for organizations, as it allows leaders to put maximum focus on performance evaluation and development — without having to try to accomplish both at the same time.

Managing Performance across National Boundaries

The evidence-based performance management approaches discussed above may be used to augment the basic process; however, the relevance and effectiveness of these practices may vary depending on the employees' work context. Unique work circumstances (e.g., expatriate managers) may require modifications to existing performance management approaches. Although these work arrangements present some novel challenges for performance management, they by no means require an overhaul of existing best practices.

In examining the performance management processes for expatriate managers and managers working exclusively in their home country, researchers have found a number of unique challenges. Specifically, these managers may experience the following obstacles:

- Difficulty in goal-setting due to conflicting interests or priorities between their new team and their "home" organization
- Limited opportunities to "view" performance

- Appraisals based solely on results, with no focus on behaviors
- Lack of appropriate feedback and performance appraisal — physical distance between expatriate managers and their supervisors may hinder communication and create challenges when providing relevant performance feedback
- Weak linkages between their performance and pay
- Limited training and development opportunities

Some researchers suggest that to compensate for the lack of face-time, more frequent reviews and regular check-ins could be conducted to mitigate these issues. Though these suggestions seem reasonable, recent studies suggest that the differential treatment of expatriates, telecommuters, and virtual workers may ultimately result in reduced job performance because they feel as if they are being micromanaged or monitored more closely than their "home office" peers.[7] Instead, managers should be encouraged to make communication with their subordinates a priority, utilizing multiple communication channels (e.g., electronic, face-to-face, or telephone) with all employees. These efforts are critical to the effectiveness of organizational performance management processes regardless of the type of employees with which managers are working. Indeed, effective organizations are differentiated not by their specific performance management practices but instead by the prevalence of active leader support and the extent to which leaders across the organization champion established processes.

Building a Business-Focused Performance Management Process

The performance management process can be a strong tool for leaders to manage the organization and drive business results. However, it does carry the risk of becoming a dreaded paper job that has to be completed once a year. We will now focus on some approaches that will make your performance management process more meaningful and business-focused.

Linkage/Gap Analysis

The performance management process can help drive the business by uncovering gaps in "how" work is done. You will want not only to assess performance on objective measures in the performance management process but also to have the manager and each employee rate the key competencies (see Chapter 3 on competency modeling). Armed with this data and the basic analytic techniques discussed below, you can uncover opportunities to make improvements:

- *Organization-wide gap analysis.* Although the performance management process is focused on the individual, it offers HR leaders a great opportunity to view the information holistically and glean critical information that can drive the business. Using "how" performance ratings, you can identify the competencies that are underperforming compared to other competencies. You can also find the competencies that are underperforming in general, from the perspective of managers. In addition, performance awareness issues may be apparent, as evidenced by significant differences between how employees and managers rate the same competencies. All of these organization-wide analyses can feed into your training needs assessment. By reviewing competency ratings at the organizational level, you can begin to create a strong training plan that is driven by real data and real needs. The lowest scoring competencies (especially those that matter most to the business) would be a great place to begin the training discussion.

- *Functional gap analysis.* For this analysis, take the same approach as the organization-wide gap analysis, except look at data from specific functions (for example, sales or finance). This approach will allow you to focus on the more specific functional competencies and on the potential deficiencies. Again, the gaps uncovered will allow you to focus on a data-driven development plan to fill the gaps. If you use an outside vendor for your performance management system, the vendor should be able to provide you with this type of function-specific data.

- *Linkage analysis.* This critical step is where the performance management ratings are statistically linked, through various methodologies, to the objective performance outcomes. Structural equation modeling is the preferred analytic solution because it allows us to identify particular performance management competencies as cause-and-effect drivers of increased performance. This implied cause-effect relationship is necessary for understanding how these different measurements relate to each other as well as for calculating an expected return on investment (ROI) for future initiatives. The approach here is to take all the competency ratings from the performance management system and align them in a spreadsheet with the performance goal (for example, "percent-achievement") numbers. The ensuing analytics will tell you which competencies are having the biggest impact on goal achievement. Having a strong understanding of the most important competencies will help HR leaders identify the specific areas in which training/development investments should be made to maximize ROI.

These three analytical steps will allow your organization to focus organization-wide training/development initiatives as well as front-line manager action plans on competencies that have a direct impact on business outcomes. The strategy that the organization can take is to have systemic initiatives but also train managers on how to examine their own data to look for gaps. This strategy will allow action plans across the organization to focus on systemic competency gaps.

From a practical perspective, working with key stakeholders on the front end to identify the types of performance analyses they would like to see conducted is valuable. Functional-focused analysis and organization-wide analysis make sense for almost any organization. Depending on your organization, those stakeholders may need the data sliced and diced in different ways (for example, by specific departments or geography). Again, an outside vendor should be able to provide you with this information. Additionally, when reporting results to senior leaders, try not to focus exclusively on participation rates but also to include a discussion of competency gaps (i.e., areas in which competency deficiencies exist) and the potential business impact of focusing on competency development across the organization.

Having data-driven solutions that have a known business impact — and a defined return on investment — will enhance the credibility of the performance management process and provide organizational leaders with a better understanding of the critical priorities that will drive the desired business outcomes.

Connecting Performance Ratings to Compensation

In our experience, a common credibility-killer of the performance management process is when employees believe that the process lacks teeth and is not directly connected to the raises they receive (i.e. the process is simply a paper job). Organizations must have defined standards for calculating performance ratings and determining subsequent pay raises. The higher the performance rating or level of goal achievement, the higher the merit increase. Even though organizations may have this approach in place, it can sometimes be sidestepped. Some basic validation of the performance ratings is necessary to establish or reestablish the credibility of the process. The procedure to accomplish this is to take the overall performance rating for each employee and line it up with the percent raise they received. A correlation analysis is sufficient to validate whether a direct connection exists between overall performance ratings and raises. A significant, positive correlation is what you are looking for in the analysis. If you do not find a significant, positive correlation, the next step would be to do some investigative work, which may involve breaking out the data by function or even location to discover any "culprits" who are not following the spirit of the system. Alternatively, it may require an organization-wide review that includes additional policy communication and training around goal-setting and performance assessment.

The great thing about the linkage analysis is that any outcome measure can be utilized in the analysis. Retention could also be examined, using historical data, to see if you were losing high performers at a greater pace than low performers. Deeper analysis could then uncover certain departments that were losing high performers at a faster rate than other departments.

The key objective is to demonstrate the business value of the performance management process — to identify it is a valid predictor of performance and the consequences (i.e. pay raise or bonus) of that performance.

Making the performance management process more business-focused allows HR leaders to make more strategic decisions and plans for employee development. In a broader sense, the foundation of performance management — which is the interaction between manager and employee — is absolutely critical to the well-being of the organization. The performance assessment provides the foundation for coaching, especially for poor performers who have the potential to improve. If such improvement does not occur and the employee is ultimately terminated, the performance assessment helps minimize legal risk by providing evidence that the termination was based on a sound, validated approach to performance management.

Practical Tips

- Do not assume that all managers know how to deliver a quality performance discussion. Provide as much training as possible to help these leaders deliver the right messages.
- When building goals, have managers make that process as collaborative as possible so that buy-in is maximized across the workforce.
- Leverage the data collected in the process to validate the impact of competencies on business outcomes and to confirm that merit increase decisions are based on actual performance ratings.
- Provide managers with rating training that focuses on avoiding rating inflation, halo error, and other distortions.
- Annually examine the inner workings of the process — from what is rated to what should be included — to maximize its effectiveness.

CHAPTER 5

Multi-rater/360 Assessments

Multi-rater assessments, often referred to as 360-degree assessments, are used by many organizations to provide employees with feedback about their job performance from a variety of sources (e.g., managers, peers, employees, self, and customers). Each of the different rating sources provides unique perspectives and information about the employee's performance, thus enhancing the validity of the performance evaluation process and helping the leader to more accurately identify the employee's strengths and weaknesses and take developmental action.[1] Multi-rater assessments have grown in popularity over the past decade; some studies have suggested that more than one-third of companies in the United States use multi-rater feedback for developmental or appraisal purposes, and this number continues to grow.[2] As multi-rater assessments become an increasingly common component of organizations' performance management systems and leadership development programs, it is beneficial to examine the features of the process that make these assessments effective as well as some common missteps that can lead to unintended and incorrect results. In this chapter, we first define multi-rater assessments and then review the process for using such assessments to drive critical business outcomes. The chapter concludes with a business-focused case study.

What the Research Tells Us

Multi-rater assessments are an integral component of many organizations' approaches to managing and developing performance — 41 percent conduct them on an annual basis.[3] These assessments provide employees with performance feedback from their supervisors, peers, customers, and direct reports. In addition, most multi-rater tools include a self-assessment component. The extent to which self-ratings and other ratings are aligned or are in agreement has been shown to have relevant implications for managerial performance.[4] The variety of feedback sources differentiates multi-rater assessments from the more traditional top-down feedback practices. If multi-rater assessments are well implemented, the range of information gleaned from them can provide managers with valuable insights into the areas in which performance is below expectation and behavioral change is necessary. Multi-rater assessments have also been used to help build teams (that is, by making team members more accountable to one another), enhance career development initiatives, and identify organizational training needs.[5]

In response to increasing competitive pressures, many organizations have moved toward a more nimble matrix structure with individuals reporting to multiple people.[6] This type of structure increases the range of people with whom individuals interact on a regular basis and often creates some ambiguity around individuals' job responsibilities and performance expectations and muddies the lines of accountability. In such environments, multi-rater assessments are more effective than traditional, top-down assessments because they provide individuals with performance feedback that captures the complex, multifaceted nature of their role. Additionally, multi-rater processes are uniquely positioned to provide feedback from key stakeholders (e.g., peers, direct reports, and managers), thus providing a more holistic performance perspective than the traditional top-down performance review.

If poorly implemented, multi-rater assessments will not have the desired effect on individual and organizational performance. Indeed, if the feedback is not solicited and delivered with care, it has the potential to hurt the recipient and hinder future performance improvement efforts.[7] To be most useful, multi-rater feedback should focus on aspects of employee behavior that can be changed and should be delivered with sensitivity. Additionally, multi-rater assessment tools have been found to fail if they are not well aligned with the organization's mission and strategic goals. Specifically, for multi-rater assessments to be effective, the results and behaviors on which people are rated must be connected to the overall strategic aims of the organization.[8]

The Benefits of Multi-Rater Processes

Over time, multi-rater/360 processes have earned a relatively positive reputation due to several advantages that are recognized by experts and consumers alike. Below, we discuss five particular benefits of the multi-rater assessment process over traditional, top-down performance appraisal systems.

Accuracy

Multi-rater assessments are more accurate than traditional, top-down performance reviews for several reasons. Ratings from multiple perspectives (e.g., self, manager, peers, and customers) provide a more accurate performance picture than relying on a single individual's point of view. Additionally, the anonymity that should be assured to raters results in more honest feedback and helps improve the accuracy of the ratings.

Face Validity

Multi-rater feedback tends to be more accepted by participants than manager evaluations alone because the performance ratings they receive are often more face valid (see Appendix A for a discussion of face validity). Employees understand that their managers are not around to observe their performance personally in every aspect of their job. Thus, having input from customers, peers, and subordinates reduces the anxiety of the "lone rater" and helps ensure that the employees' performance across all aspects of their jobs is considered.

Richer Insights

Providing feedback from multiple perspectives not only improves accuracy and acceptance, but it also provides participants with valuable insight into how their performance is perceived by different groups of stakeholders. People behave differently when interacting with different stakeholders, whose perceptions of the same behavior may vary. Understanding these differences across stakeholders can be very insightful for employees. These insights provide valuable information for changing behaviors and improving perceptions of essential stakeholder groups.

Open Communication

Another benefit of multi-rater surveys is that they help improve communication about performance. Encouraging all stakeholders to be involved in the giving and receiving of feedback helps make performance more openly discussed. This sharing of performance feedback eventually becomes part of the organizational culture and provides participants with the opportunity to speak openly regarding performance with their managers and other key stakeholders (for example, peers and direct reports).

Practical and Cost Effective

Multi-rater assessments are usually cost-effective and widely available online or as software that has made them easier to implement and interpret. The cost per participant is extremely low considering the individual- and organizational-level applications of the assessment results.[9]

Effective Execution

A wealth of research has examined how to effectively implement a multi-rater assessment process. An actionable summary of the research and specific recommendations are required to help HR practitioners implement or improve their multi-rater/360 process.[10] To this end, we have organized the research into 15 execution-focused topics.

Assess Organizational Readiness/Identify Champions

When considering implementing a multi-rater/360 assessment, consider the current organizational environment as well as the organization's performance management history. To maximize their effectiveness, multi-rater assessments must be implemented at an appropriate time. If, for example, the assessment is implemented during a stressful time, such as during organizational downsizing, employees may perceive it as a tool to use in determining future workforce cuts. The developmental intentions of the assessment will likely not be realized, and employee morale and trust in the organization may be further harmed.

Also consider the specific timing of the multi-rater assessment process and ensure that it is aligned with other organization-wide systems and processes (for example, the execution of internal employee moves or employee surveys).The individuals who will be raters in this process will need to have observed "in action" the person being rated for at least six months before being able to offer an informed performance assessment. Additionally, HR departments in large organizations may have one part of the function responsible for the multi-rater assessment, while another part may be responsible for the employee opinion survey. Conducting the employee opinion survey and the multi-rater assessment simultaneously, or in close proximity, may seem appropriate, as you will have everyone's attention. However, over-surveying the population is very detrimental and will not only impact your participation rates but, more importantly, will have a negative impact on how deeply the data is digested and acted upon within the organization.

Finally, HR leaders should understand the organization's history prior to implementing a new performance assessment process. Reviewing previous attempts to institute similar performance assessment processes and examining their circumstances and timing provides insights into what went right and what went wrong. Interviews with current stakeholders, as well as with those who were involved in any prior efforts, will help illuminate potential challenges and resistance and will elicit critical buy-in from key individuals prior to rolling out a new initiative. An opportune time to do this type of research is when you are conducting the stakeholder interviews at the first step in the Business Partner RoadMap™ (see Chapter 1). During the stakeholder interviews, HR leaders should talk about (and answer questions about) the additional capabilities of the multi-rater assessment process (for example, systemic and linkage analyses) and begin to obtain critical buy-in from leaders at all levels. Including both senior leaders and front-line managers from across the organization in the stakeholder interview process is crucial. Senior leaders will help ensure the program's success by personally championing the assessment initiative and communicating this commitment to others. Front-line managers may serve a similar role, acting as program champions and ensuring that the assessment processes are appropriately implemented and well understood within their span of control.

Communicate Clear Objectives and Intended Outcomes

For those who lack confidence in their job abilities or are uncertain about their job security, honest and direct feedback from multiple sources can be intimidating. Therefore, communicating to employees the purpose of the multi-rater assessment system is essential. Specifically, managers should communicate both the ways in which individuals will benefit by participating and the impact the process will ultimately have on the organization (for example, by enhancing accountability and improving individual and organizational performance). Participants should clearly understand the way in which the assessment results will be used. Is the assessment purely developmental, or will the results be used to make substantial HR decisions (for example, awarding bonuses or promotions)? Executive champions can help set the tone for the multi-rater assessment, communicating the business need and the developmental benefits individuals can expect through their participation in the process. Front-line managers should then reinforce this message by responding to employee concerns and emphasizing the developmental nature of the assessment process.

Integrate with Existing Programs

Multi-rater assessments are just one component of a year-round performance planning and review process, which also includes such components as individual goal-setting, training, development, and teambuilding. To reinforce this message, multi-rater assessments should be well integrated with existing HR practices. For instance, multi-rater assessment data may be used to identify gaps in managerial competencies, thereby informing and improving training and development practices. Additionally, the feedback that individuals receive as part of the multi-rater assessment process may be used as the foundation for career-development conversations and succession planning initiatives. Such alignment will help reinforce the goals of the assessment process and establish it as an integral component of the organization's overall culture and performance management system. Vendors generally have the capability to seamlessly link multi-rater assessment results into performance management systems.

Ensure Reliability and Validity of the Instrument

Although assessing validity and reliability of feedback instruments is critical to the process, organizations rarely take the time to ensure this occurs. Multi-rater assessments are often used purely for developmental purposes, which has unfortunately created the assumption that they do not need to be rigorously evaluated for validity and reliability.[11] Ironically, if multi-rater assessments were going to be used to make

HR decisions (e.g., hiring, promotion, and termination), their validity and reliability would be at the forefront of leaders' concerns. (Refer to Appendix A for a complete discussion of reliability and validity.) Below we outline several issues that are specific to multi-rater assessments.

A few key areas need to be assessed before either building a multi-rater assessment instrument yourself or purchasing an instrument from a vendor. First, you will want to make sure that your organization has a validated competency model, as this will serve as the foundation for the multi-rater assessment (see Chapter 3 for a detailed discussion of competency modeling). The questions or dimensions included on the multi-rater assessment should come directly from the validated competency model. This practice helps ensure the credibility of the process in the eyes of participants and the relevance of the performance feedback. Second, prior to organization-wide implementation, the multi-rater assessment should be piloted with a sample of willing participants, thus allowing you to assess the validity and reliability of the instrument before it is widely distributed.

Finally, the validity of the process can often be enhanced by allowing raters to respond to open-ended questions regarding the feedback recipient's performance. Deciding how many open-ended items to include on the assessment is not an exact science; however, in our practical experience we have found three or fewer open-ended items to suffice. In particular, we recommend including an open-ended item that focuses the rater's attention on providing one piece of feedback to help the recipient improve his or her performance.

Clarify the Roles and Responsibilities of Those Involved

Many individuals, including HR professionals and line managers, are involved in the design and implementation of a multi-rater assessment system. With so many interested stakeholders and the inherent interdependence of the tasks to be executed, everyone involved must understand their responsibilities. Determine in advance who will be responsible for administering feedback and the format through which performance feedback will be delivered (for example, one-on-one, in facilitated sessions, or in group sessions). In addition, the employees themselves must be clear about the role they play in the process. Clarifying such roles and responsibilities up front will prevent important aspects from being forgotten once the assessment process has been implemented.

Select and Train Raters

Feedback recipients will need to select certain raters in the process, particularly peers and customers. The selection of raters is significant; therefore, providing training on making appropriate selections will help to facilitate success. For peers, feedback recipients should select individuals with whom they have had a substantial amount of interaction across various situations and who can provide an honest, informed assessment of their performance. Selecting "friends" who may be likely to give favorable, but not necessarily accurate ratings, is not acceptable. Additionally, feedback recipients should avoid selecting raters who may have a conflict of interest, such as raters who are applying for the same promotion. Organizations can prevent this situation by having managers vet employees' rater lists and add or delete raters as they see appropriate. Feedback recipients should also select a variety of customer raters who have an extended track record of working with them but who are not only their "best" customers (see Figure 5.1). Managers can get involved by requiring certain customers, based on size or activity levels, to be on the list or by making geography-based selections if possible. Customers should be informed upfront that the feedback they provide will be 100 percent anonymous. Of course feedback recipients want to score well on the multi-rater assessment; however, if the developmental objectives are made clear and they realize the upside of getting honest versus good feedback, then feedback recipients will take a more thoughtful approach to selecting raters.

Figure 5.1 Tips for Increasing Customer Responses

1. Employees should personally invite customers to provide feedback, communicating the following:
    - » Emphasize the organization's continuous efforts to improve customer service, meet customers' needs and gather customer feedback and input
    - » The organization and the employee value his/her input
    - » His/Her feedback will be used to improve the employee's performance, as well as guide organizational development at a macro-level
    - » Confirm the contact information of the customer
2. After the survey process is completed, employees should provide the customer with a summary of the development feedback received and the developmental activities planned to address the feedback.

The raters themselves should receive training on how to use the multi-rater assessment and accurately rate feedback recipients. Raters maybe encountering the assessment process for the first time, so clarifying the rating scale and establishing performance expectations will be beneficial. Specifically, individuals across all levels of the organization should be able to identify particular behaviors that are associated with each level of performance (for example, outstanding performance, on-target performance, and below-target performance). This level-setting process will help all raters use the rating scale in a similar manner, thus enhancing the validity of the assessment process. External customers should receive the same type of training; however, time constraints will require that the training be brief and that instructions with sample items/ratings be embedded within the assessment itself.

Align Ratings with Observable Behaviors

Aligning ratings with observable behaviors is a critical best practice that can easily get lost in the process of building and executing the multi-rater assessment process.[12] The provision of ratings from multiple sources across different levels of the organization is a key strength of the multi-rater assessment process. However, raters will vary in the degree to which they interact with the person whom they are rating. Some raters, such as the individual's manager, have frequent interaction, whereas others, like peers and customers, may only see the individual in particular settings or on specific projects. If raters who interact with the individual less frequently are asked to provide performance ratings on a multi-rater assessment, their evaluations will likely be biased by general impressions. Such biased or uninformed ratings will skew the results of the multi-rater assessment and create confusion as recipients attempt to extract meaningful feedback from their report.

Further, detailed instructions for raters should be included on the actual instrument to ensure that the instructions are fresh in raters' minds. Finally, remind all raters on multiple occasions that their ratings will be completely anonymous and that any group-level breakdowns (e.g., peers and direct reports) will only be provided if at least a pre-established minimum number of ratings have been received. This number is typically set at three or more, but it does vary based on the culture of the organization. The feedback recipient's manager is the only exception. As generally only one manager-rating occurs, HR practitioners should remind managers that their individual ratings will be seen by the feedback recipient.

Coach Employees on Interpreting Their Ratings

A common oversight is giving individual employees their assessment reports and leaving them to their own devices. Two negative situations can arise from not helping employees interpret their ratings. First, they may attempt to interpret the large amount of data and fancy charts, get frustrated, ignore the results, and not take any actions for improvement. Alternatively, they may make a valiant effort to interpret the reports (without any help), draw the wrong conclusions, and then spend time working on making improvements in areas that are not the most relevant to their overall performance. To prevent these situations, take one of the following steps: (1) meet one-on-one with all report recipients to conduct a detailed debrief of results, answer questions, and assist them in beginning to build an action plan; or (2) if the one-on-one meetings are not feasible, conduct training sessions (including webinars) for all recipients that walk them through the business case for the process, the overall organization results, a sample report, and a sample action plan and conclude with a question-and-answer session. If the multi-rater assessment was conducted only at certain levels in the organization (for example, for front-line managers only), then training the recipients' managers on the interpretation of reports will prepare them serve as an additional resources for during analysis, interpretation, and action planning.

In addition, HR leaders can help by recognizing and acknowledging for participants that receiving performance feedback, especially negative feedback, is never easy. The four-step SARA (Surprise, Anger, Rationalization, and Acceptance) outlines the typical emotional process experienced by recipients of negative feedback. Reactions to negative feedback that follows the SARA model might look like these comments:

> *Surprise:* "I cannot believe that I scored low in these three areas. These are the things I work the hardest on."
> *Anger:* "Who rated me this way? This is ridiculous — this assessment tool cannot be accurate!"
> *Rationalization:* "I bet this was those two folks over in accounting. I held them accountable for their actions a few years ago, and they never got over it."
> *Acceptance:* "I guess the numbers don't lie. If this is what people perceive, then I must need to try harder or try something different in my low-scoring areas."

Discussing SARA with feedback recipients upfront is an effective way to help them move quickly through the early stages. Only when they reach Acceptance can the development and action planning processes begin in earnest. Informing the managers of feedback recipients of the SARA model is wise so that they can prepare to deal with the recipients' reactions.

Train Employees on Creating Development Plans

Following through on the results is critical to the overall success of the process. Even if recipients get their feedback, analyze it, and understand where they should spend their time, the results will be of limited value without a personal development plan for them to work with throughout the year. We cannot assume that all employees know how to create effective development plans. Feedback recipients should be trained on how to build and execute against their development plans. In addition, the managers of feedback recipients should learn how to assist their employees in building appropriate development plans and hold them accountable for achieving their developmental goals. (See Chapter 8 for a more thorough discussion of building development plans.)

Formalize a Goal-Setting Component

Incorporating goal-setting into the process increases the likelihood that employees' performance will improve over a designated period of time.[13] Challenging goals help hold feedback recipients accountable for desired performance improvement over a designated period of time and reinforce the message that the multi-rater assessment is just one part of a year-round performance improvement process. Performance goals should help clarify work priorities and establish an objective metric for measuring performance improvement. The most effective performance goals follow the SMART approach outlined in Table 5.1.[14]

Table 5.1

SMART Goal-Setting Criteria	Definition	Example
Specific	Performance goals should clearly state what is to be accomplished in terms of the end results; they are not simply a list of the tasks required to accomplish the end result.	Focus on Product ABC.....
Measurable	Goals should clearly state the level of accomplishment that is expected; achievement of the performance goal should be observable through quantitative and/or qualitative measures.	....to sell $1 million worth....
Action Verb	Performance goals should be written using action-oriented behavioral statements, including verbs that characterize observable behavior associated with goal accomplishment.	....following the new sales model...
Realistic	Goals should be realistic, yet challenging. Employees will be frustrated if they are responsible for activities that are beyond their span of control or cannot be achieved in a reasonable amount of time.	....versus $800k worth last year.....
Time Bound	The time period within which the goal will be accomplished should be clearly delineated; short- and long-term expectations should be differentiated.	.....by the end of July.

Implement the Process on a Routine Basis

A perplexing issue that surrounds multi-rater assessments is the assumption that they are a one-time occurrence.[15] Oftentimes, organizations start with the idea that they will implement multi-rater assessments in a given fiscal year, follow all the prescribed best-practices, and even make the process as business-focused as possible, and then...nothing. One of the keys to maximizing the effectiveness of any feedback process is the ability to show participants positive gains in the areas in which they have spent time working to improve. However, for many organizations, the prospect of repeating the multi-rater assessment the following year or maybe even 18 months down the road is not on the radar screen. Often leaders only think they need to hear feedback from multiple stakeholders once. However, these processes require a substantial time investment from all parties involved and a financial investment (we will consider ROI and business impact later in this chapter); therefore, ignoring the need for follow-up assessments and only providing one opportunity for assessment is shortsighted and, ultimately, harmful to all involved stakeholders. Conducting a systemic needs assessment and linkage analyses (as discussed in Chapter 1) improves the chances that multi-rater assessments will be viewed as a business necessity and increases the likelihood that funding will be allocated for follow-up assessments.

Use the Multi-Rater Assessment for Development Purposes Only

One of the more controversial issues surrounding multi-rater assessment processes is the question of whether to use them exclusively for development or to use them to make HR decisions. Research consistently comes down on the side of using this process for development purposes only.[16] The reasons primarily focus on the quality and accuracy of the ratings that will be received. When multi-rater assessments are used to make significant HR decisions (for example, promotions), participants are likely to select raters who will provide inflated performance ratings, thus compromising the integrity of the assessment process. If used for development purposes, participants will tend to select a broader range of raters, and the raters themselves will be more focused on providing honest responses.[17]

Additionally, the interpretation of rating discrepancies between stakeholder groups (for example, self, manager, and peers) has been found to vary depending on the purpose of the assessment. When used for development, employees are often encouraged to explore the rating discrepancies, thus helping them to become more self-aware.[18] However, when compensation or promotion decisions are on the line, employees may become defensive or hostile, inappropriately pursue clarification from various stakeholders, and fail to become more self-aware as a result of the feedback.[19] Thus communicating to participants, early and often, that the assessment process will be used for development purposes only is important, as they likely will not assume that this is the case.

Present the Assessment Data in Multiple Formats

HR practitioners should present the data from the multi-rater assessment in multiple formats. Some people are very visual and respond better to charts or graphs, while others are numbers-driven and like to see the aggregated performance ratings provided by each group of raters. Using multiple formats will help your internal customers (i.e., the employees being rated and their managers) readily digest the results of the multi-rater assessment. It will also weaken any excuses or rationalizations as to why the data were not understood and/or actions were not taken based on the results.

Focus on Task/Skills Improvement

The results of the multi-rater assessment and the follow-up feedback should always focus on tasks related to the job and not on the person or the personality of the feedback recipient.

According to research:

> If feedback focuses attention at the level of the self because it is personalized, or because the task in question is closely related to the person's self-concept, subsequent performance will typically suffer, as the person's attention will be distracted from task improvement.[20]

Below is an example of task- and skill-focused feedback:

> "Manager: This position requires an employee to be able to clearly communicate complex information, accurately analyze data, and balance risk and reward in decision-making. Based on the feedback we received from your colleagues and customers, at this point you are proficient in the first two competencies but could use some training to bolster your decision-making ability."

Similarly, when presenting information in your feedback reports, focus the recipients' attention on their own data and provide information relevant to identifying their strengths as well as their opportunities for development. What should be minimized in the discussion of ratings is how an individual's performance specifically compares to another's performance. Once the multi-rater assessment becomes a competition among the recipients, the focus on what is important — individual improvement — is diminished. In this instance, competition is not a good thing and will often paint an incorrect picture of developmental needs. This is not to suggest that department ratings or similar roll-ups should be withheld, as these can help individual employees understand how they scored relative to their peers. However, the mere fact that a person scored lower than a peer does not represent an automatic weakness or urgent need to "fix" that situation. We need to acknowledge any discrepancy but place our attention on key areas of task and behavioral deficiencies as the basis for development.

Evaluate the Effectiveness of the Entire Multi-Rater Assessment Process

Prior to implementing a multi-rater assessment, success metrics (for example, individual performance improvement and departmental or organizational performance improvement) need to be determined and built into an evaluation of the assessment process. The goal of the evaluation is to uncover any areas of the assessment process — from assessment tools and technologies to follow-up coaching and action planning — that may be in need of revision or improvement. Often, assessment takes the form of surveys, interviews, and observations of participants in the process. To ensure that assessment results are acted upon, an implementation team comprised of managers and HR professionals is often appointed to gather feedback, derive conclusions, and implement solutions. The most useful evaluations go beyond simply gauging satisfaction with the process and instead link the process to meaningful business outcomes (for example, individual performance improvement or market share). In addition, data from multi-rater assessments should be used to conduct systemic training needs assessments. In the next section, we discuss our process for linking the multi-rater assessment to critical business outcomes.

Building a Business-Focused Multi-Rater/360 Process

As is the case with many HR practices, the effectiveness of multi-source assessments is rarely demonstrated in quantifiable terms.[21] Organizational leaders often stop short, evaluating satisfaction with the multi-rater assessment process but missing the opportunity to link what is rated on multi-rater assessments to business outcomes. Looking only at satisfaction with the process devalues the multi-rater assessment in the eyes of executive-level decision-makers who, in lieu of a demonstrated return on investment, are likely to cut funding when faced with budget constraints.

Two opportunities exist to make this process more directly focused on business outcomes. First, organizations can follow the approach outlined in Chapter 1 (the Business Partner RoadMap™) to identify the cause-and-effect relationship between the specific skills, knowledge, and behaviors that were measured during the multi-rater assessment process and critical business outcomes. To demonstrate the link to business outcomes, first obtain the appropriate data at the appropriate level (e.g., manager level or workgroup level). This means that the multi-rater assessment data are measured at the same level and during the same timeframe as the business outcome data (for example, unit-level performance numbers). The data used should be function or workgroup specific. For example, if "sales dollars" has been identified as a critical business outcome for the sales team, you will incorporate and statistically link the sales function's multi-rater assessment data to the "sales dollars" outcome. Or if you are examining customer service satisfaction ratings as a business outcome, you will pull in just the multi-rater assessment data from the customer service centers and link this data to customer satisfaction. Using structural equation modeling as your analytical methodology, you can identify which components of the multi-rater assessment (i.e., which knowledge, skills, and abilities) are key drivers of specific business outcomes for the various functions or workgroups being analyzed. Specifically, the results of the analysis indicate the differential impact that each of the competencies assessed using the multi-rater assessment has on the key business outcome (i.e., how much improvements on each competency will contribute to improvements in the overall business outcome). Discovering the competencies most responsible for business outcomes allows HR leaders to make data-driven decisions regarding where to invest developmental efforts and dollars and to demonstrate a return on these investments on the back end. The following case study exemplifies this process, highlighting the way in which multi-rater assessments can become critical business drivers.

Case Study: Pharmaceutical Sales Force

The sales leadership at a small pharmaceutical company wanted to invest in the individual development of its specialty sales representatives and identify the critical skills needed to gain market share on its primary competitor. The company's brand possessed a 23.3 percent market share. This particular market was relatively mature, and the organization's leaders were looking for a new commercial edge in an extremely competitive environment. Table 5.2 reveals the broader challenges facing the organization.

Table 5.2 Challenges Facing the Organization

Investing in the development of its specialty pharmaceutical sales representatives
Identifying the critical skills for its sales representatives
Growing market share in a competitive, mature market
Understanding the ROI of its training investments
Revenue growth

Implementing the Selling Skills 360

Organizational leaders (with the help of the HR function) decided to implement a development-focused multi-rater assessment initiative. The performance ratings would be used to identify strengths and development opportunities among the sales force, but the results were not linked to personnel decisions. The purpose was to build trust in the process and to encourage sales representative participation. To reinforce this message, individual reports were delivered solely to the sales representative. However, sales representatives were encouraged to share the results with their manager, thereby allowing them to leverage the coaching process and development tools made available to them.

Assessing Sales Representative Competencies

The multi-rater assessment consisted of 25 skill and behavior-based items representing seven sales representative competencies:

- Account Management
- Core Selling Skills
- Relationship Building
- Consultative Selling
- Product & Disease-State Expertise
- Evidence-Based Selling®
- Managed-Care Expertise

In addition, managers and physicians could provide recommendations for improvement for the sales representative in an open-ended item. Physicians were identified by the organization based on territory market-share potential. Each sales representative then personally invited individual physicians to complete the short online survey (no incentive was offered to physicians to complete the survey). Managers completed an assessment of the same competencies for each sales representative. Finally, each representative completed a self-assessment, also of the same competencies, to aid in the development planning process.

Assessment Participation

A total of 116 sales representatives participated in the business-focused multi-rater assessment. Survey invitations were mailed to over 1,200 physicians, and more than 50 percent responded. On average, 7.5 responses were received for each sales representative, including 5.5 physician responses, a manager response, and a self-assessment.

Sales Representatives and Manager Results

Individual sales representatives were each provided with a summary report of their assessment results. A feedback workshop was delivered to sales representatives and managers to assist them in understanding the reports, identifying strengths and development opportunities, building a development plan, and leveraging the information within the organization's existing field-coaching process.

Managers received a summary report for their specific territories — which typically included 8-10 sales representatives. This report allowed individual managers to follow a similar development planning process focused on their local sales team.

Organizational Results

Using the aggregated multi-rater assessment data, we conducted an overall, systemic analysis. Sales representatives' competencies were examined as drivers of territory market share, which was identified as the primary business outcome for each sales representative. Manager and physician responses were linked to the previous six-month territory market share for each sales representative. The results of the linkage analysis are depicted in Figure 5.2. This analysis allowed the organization to prioritize initiatives around the individual behaviors that had a cause-and-effect impact on the desired outcome (i.e., market share).

Figure 5.2 Cause-and-Effect Drivers of Pharmaceutical Market Share

Expected ROI and Project Applications

The systemic analysis allowed the sales organization to assess current sales representatives' capabilities and prioritize training and development interventions. Furthermore, the organization estimated that an improvement in its Evidence-Based Selling® score of 0.24 (in other words, nearly one-fourth of a standard deviation) would increase revenue by $4.5 million annually. To address key needs in the areas of Evidence-Based Selling® and Product & Disease-State Expertise, the organization planned training interventions for all sales representatives. The expected ROI calculation was used to secure funding for the subsequent training interventions.

In addition to the impact on the organization's training strategy, the results of the study were used to adjust the brand strategy of the product. Overall, the results of the Selling Skills multi-rater assessment were found to have numerous applications and impacts across the organization.

Results

Pharmaceutical sales increased by over $5 million annually after the training interventions were fully executed — showing the power of using analytics to focus on the competencies that are driving business outcomes. The sales function now looks to human resources to discover new areas in which to focus to gain market share for all their products.

This initiative was a strong opportunity for the HR function to work collaboratively with another function in the organization and to demonstrate a positive impact on a critical business outcome (prescription market share). As the sales force at this organization moves forward in its quest to gain market share, business-focused HR practices and processes continue to play a prominent role.

Practical Tips

- Communicate, and be transparent, about the goals of conducting a multi-rater assessment; use multiple forms and venues to communicate leading up to the assessment launch.
- Share upfront how the data will be used to draw linkages to important business outcomes; this practice will increase buy-in for the process.
- Provide as much individual and group training as possible on how to interpret the results, and use them to create development plans.
- Train leaders on how to deliver the results effectively to their employees.
- Include items on the assessment that have received key stakeholder input and are customized to your organization.
- Use analytics to link the items on the assessment to critical business outcomes.
- Share the results of the linkage analyses with stakeholders across the organization to ensure that all leaders understand the business impact of the process.

Employee Opinion Surveys

Employee opinion surveys, if done right, are *management* tools that allow the organization's leadership team to recruit and retain top talent, to stay or become competitive in the marketplace, and to deliver on financial goals. Human resources is often the driver of this critical tool. Recent findings show that nearly 80 percent of mid-to-large organizations conduct these surveys on a somewhat regular basis (biannually or annually).[1] Conducting surveys offers many advantages, from identifying areas of concern to pinpointing areas of strength to leverage. However, effective survey execution can be elusive for many organizations, and using the data to actually drive business outcomes is even more uncommon.

In this chapter, we will review what the latest applied research tells us about surveys and how to execute the process effectively. In addition we will discuss ways of using analytics to build the business case for systemic action and to ensure that your employee survey is business-focused.

What the Research Tells Us

When constructing a survey, applied research provides us with many useful and practical guidelines to follow. Building and executing employee surveys is both art and science. We will weave together both applied research and the practical knowledge gained from our years of experience in putting successful survey processes in place.

Before we jump into the research, a couple of points are worth mentioning. First, the research we will review is primarily focused on methodological considerations (e.g., how to conduct employee opinion surveys). Employee surveys were developed for organizations to understand the unique needs of their employees. Although looking across survey responses at different organizations can be useful for identifying trends and benchmarking performance, this approach often detracts from efforts to understand the unique factors that drive employee satisfaction and engagement within an organization. The bottom line is that organizations and people are complex and complicated. So instead of providing some simple, universal tool, we are going to review the research that will help you create a valid and practical tool to diagnose the most pressing issues facing your own organization.

Second, there is plenty of confusion regarding what employee opinion surveys measure — is it satisfaction, commitment, loyalty, engagement? The truth is that these different labels are more a creation of survey vendors' marketing departments than true distinctions relevant to practice. Oftentimes survey vendors rebrand their instruments without really changing the content. It is true that concepts such as engagement and "organizational citizenship behaviors" (i.e., going above and beyond the requirements of your job) have focused more on extra-role behaviors.[2] Measuring this outcome with a survey is useful; however, it does not replace the need to assess employee loyalty or satisfaction. So in reality, a survey should measure engagement, loyalty, commitment, and satisfaction. Applied research has validated this idea that engagement is simply part of the measurement category — not some completely new concept. Do not get too caught up in what you call the survey. Instead, focus more on implementing a *valid* and *practical* survey. To this end, we will focus more on methodological research and advice than on summarizing what research suggests are the key drivers of satisfaction. To get the most out of the survey process, you will need to determine which employee attitudes are driving satisfaction in your organization — and we will show you how to do so.

Effective Design and Execution

The items included on any employee survey are obviously significant. Whether you use a survey vendor or write your own items, certain practices will maximize the effectiveness of the process. First, when writing items, make sure they are single-barreled, that is, that they ask only one question at a time. A double-barreled item would be "My manager is a strategic thinker *and* a good communicator." The problem with this item is that you are asking for two ratings in one item. What if the manager is a strategic thinker but a poor communicator? What if the manager is a good communicator but a poor strategic thinker? As you can see, properly answering a double-barreled survey item is nearly impossible. And interpreting and measuring responses is equally futile.[3]

The second area is the number of items to include in a survey. If we assume that we are discussing an annual, organization-wide survey, then the length should fall between 35-60 items. This is not a magic number, but one based on our experience. Once an individual has spent 15 minutes on a computer answering survey questions, fatigue sets in and inevitable distractions arise. In addition, hourly employees are typically on the clock when taking the survey, so costs will mount if the survey is too long. On the other hand, a survey that is too short will not be as comprehensive, and the results will be less actionable.[4] For example, a popular 12-item survey is available through a national consulting firm. This short survey purports to tell you how "engaged" your organization is, but it is very difficult for a local manager to use the results to create a specific action plan with any level of confidence. Additionally, imagining that only a dozen questions can capture a sufficient cross-section of the work environment and work experiences of employees is difficult.

The same thought process should be followed using open-ended items on a survey. Yes, allowing employees to include comments on a survey does provide rich data; however, open-ended items require more time for employees to complete and increase the complexity associated with interpreting and reporting the results. With that in mind, limit the number of open-ended items to three. You also need to ensure strict confidentiality on the survey if you want to receive frank responses, particularly on the open-ended items. The open-ended items can be very broad (e.g. "What is the one thing you would do to make this organization a better place to work?") or very specific (e.g. "How is this organization managing the new product development process?"). We recommend asking one of each type so that you permit and encourage employees to speak freely but also focus them in on a topic that needs a direct answer. Further, the HR department should at a minimum "scrub" the open-ended comments of any individuals' names or identifying information before presenting the results. This step will help safeguard the confidentiality of participants and protect those who may have been criticized or attacked in the open-ended feedback.

The response/rating scale you use for the survey items is very important, and research has informed us of a right way and a wrong way to construct them.[5] The preferred approach is to use a "Likert-type" rating scale (that is, Strongly Agree through Strongly Disagree). We (supported by research) recommend using a 5-point Likert Scale format. For example:

Strongly Agree — Agree — Neutral — Disagree — Strongly Disagree
or
Very Satisfied — Satisfied — Neutral — Dissatisfied — Very Dissatisfied

Studies suggest that a 7-point response scale produces equally valid and reliable results; however, no additional variance is captured when more than five points are included on the scale. The key is to use an odd number of response options, thus providing respondents with a midpoint or neutral choice (as we discuss in greater detail below). Also essential is not to provide respondents with too many options, as vast research suggests that individuals cannot effectively process more than 10 points of distinction on a Likert Scale (for example, is there a real difference between a rating of eight and nine on a 10-point scale?).[6] On the other hand, too few response options (e.g., a 3-point scale) can limit the usefulness of the responses and prevent you from distinguishing between "satisfied" and "highly satisfied" employees. Keep in mind that the only valid reason to add more points to your scale is to capture more variance or nuance in the responses.

Managers typically have concerns about including a "neutral" rating in the rating scale. Many want to force employees to "take sides." This is a fair concern. Consistent with existing research, we counsel in favor of the "neutral" rating (or inclusion of an N/A option) for a few reasons:

- Forcing employees to pick a side will either lead to artificially high or artificially low scores, instead of accurate scores.

- You may have relatively new employees who have not dealt with, for example, their benefits plan yet and cannot make any type of rating.

- If a manager has behaved poorly in the eyes of employees but has recently started to turn the corner, employees may not be "sold" on a positive rating, but they are not currently feeling negative.[7]

Finally, the items you include in the survey should have "content validity" (see Appendix B for a discussion of validity and reliability). In other words, the survey you construct should include items that effectively cover all the significant aspects of employees' work environment. This recommendation does not mean that you have to cover all aspects in minute detail. However, it does mean that you should include questions about the manager, the organization as a whole, the local workgroup, and appropriate business issues. Conducting stakeholder interviews with senior leaders, managers, and employees from across numerous functions during the survey design process will help you unearth any organization-specific issues that should be included on the survey (for example, new benefit plan changes that may be a source of concern). Repeating this step each year before re-administering the survey increases the practical value of the survey (that is, it keeps the survey "fresh" and valuable).

Rates of Response

A magic response rate number that every organization should achieve does not exist. However, keep in mind some guidelines. First, assess how many responses you need in order to have a representative (i.e., valid) sample. Several online tools allow you to input the number of employees in your organization and obtain the minimum number of survey responses you will need in order to have a valid sample.[8] The average response rate is usually 60 percent to 70 percent. A lower response rate will undercut the statistical validity and organizational credibility of the results. Imagine walking into a survey follow-up meeting and announcing the results and then telling everyone that only 10 percent of the employees completed the survey. The level of buy-in for the results will likely be low. You could make the survey mandatory, which might raise response rates but could lower peoples' attitudes before they take the survey. Alternatively, you can motivate people to participate with, for example, raffle prizes — this tactic has shown to increase survey participation rates. However, the best ways to increase the response rate are to do the following:

- Take action on the results at all levels. The best way to get people to respond to the survey in the future is having a historical record of meaningful follow-up to address the results of the survey. If no effort or a meaningless effort is taken on the results, then employees will be less likely to take future surveys seriously.
- Ensure that senior leaders communicate their commitment to the process and emphasize the value of receiving employee feedback.
- Avoid over-surveying your people. HR leaders should be the gatekeepers of surveys for the organization. Although easier said than done, limiting the number of surveys employees are asked to complete will help ensure high response rates.

UPS achieves a 90 percent response rate every year, and participation in their employee survey is entirely voluntary without the use of raffles or other forms of incentive. How do they consistently obtain such a high response rate? Their survey is built into the culture of the organization, and their people know that action will be taken on the results. If you show organizational commitment to the survey by taking action on the results, you will see the response rates increase over time as employees learn to trust the process and understand its value.

Reporting Data

Providing a report to all managers with the results about their specific performance on the survey should be a key priority upon completion of any survey — with a caveat. Organizations should adopt a "less than" rule to protect participant confidentiality. If a manager or workgroup has less than a pre-established number of employees who respond to the survey, then that manager or workgroup will not receive a breakout report of the results because individual responses could be identified. We recommend four as your cut-off (but this number can be as high as 10 or as low as three). The number you select depends on your culture — if the culture has widespread trust issues, then use a higher number; if it is more collegial, then a lower number may be appropriate. The key is to gauge the comfort level of your employees before you set the number, to make sure you get it right.

The content of the survey report is highly varied. At a minimum, you will want to provide the overall survey category scores for the individual manager (for example, average or percent favorable). Providing leaders with this information for each survey item is also wise so that they can craft specific action plans. Later in this chapter, we will show you how to include business-focused analytics into local reports as well. Many organizations also have nice charts and graphs included in the reports they provide. This decision is completely up to personal taste. Nice charts are nice — but there is no proof that they stimulate action from the survey any more than a black and white report with numbers only. Use a format that is familiar to employees and provides practical, easy-to-interpret results. The goal is for managers to spend more time taking action and less time reading reports and interpreting the results.

When rolling out the survey results, utilize all feasible media to communicate with employees, and let them know that you are taking action. Some effective communication methods include the following:

- *Intranet.* An initial story with quotes/comments from the CEO about the results and a commitment to take action and follow-up.
- *E-mail.* A short note from the manager with high-level results and a commitment to set up a department meeting to review the results in more detail.
- *Newsletter.* A story with a few charts or graphs of the results and more detailed commentary about the data.

In terms of presenting the results, a vendor should present the material to the senior team and also make presentations to larger departments or sites (depending on the size of the organization). The CEO should host a company-wide town hall meeting or webinar to review the results with the leaders in the organization.

Open-Ended Survey Comments

The HR department, or survey vendor, should also summarize the open-ended comments collected in the survey. To effectively present this data to senior leaders, the comments should be summarized into categories, and the total percentage of comments within each category should be included. This approach is often referred to as a content analysis and involves identifying common themes across open-ended responses, categorizing comments within those themes, and calculating the percent of comments that fall within each theme. Figure 6.1 provides an example of themes from an open-ended question.

Figure 6.1

Please provide one suggestion on how to make this organization a better place to work.
1. Provide training and development opportunities (16%)
2. Address staffing issues (15%)
3. Open lines of communication (14%)
4. Encourage teambuilding within and across departments (10%)
5. Promote work/personal life balance (7%)
6. Emphasize accountability, fairness, and respect (4%)
7. Recognize/reward employees for their performance (6%)

Additionally, we recommend that only summaries of the open-ended comments be released to leaders. We are aware that leaders really like to read the comments — they are much more excited to pour over the comments than over a lot of numbers. However, reading comments objectively is difficult, particularly if they are about your own department. For example, in a department comprised of 1,000 employees, one comment may point out that the department is not strategic. This is just one comment out of 1,000 — hardly an overwhelming majority. However, a leader may take this single comment as a call to action or a complete indictment of the department, even if the quantitative survey results do not support this response. Alternatively, if managers have preconceived notions about the department, they may look explicitly for open-ended comments that confirm these preconceived notions, thus making them a reality. The point is that the comments tend to carry a lot of weight — typically more than the survey numbers — so they should be dealt with and distributed carefully. The same logic applies when doing a follow-up meeting about the survey or focus group — the loudest voice can dominate the conversation — but it is only one voice and may not be reflective of the entire group. This possibility is why having human resources or outside experts examine the data, summarize it, and make recommendations is a preferred methodology, when possible.

Survey vendors may also provide "normative/benchmark data," or normal/average scores for a given survey item or category across similar organizations. Normative data allows you to compare your organization's level of performance with that of other organizations in your survey vendor's database. Including normative/benchmark data is completely up to you. If your organization's senior leaders have a high level of interest in them, then ask your survey vendor to provide the data. When selecting a survey vendor, make sure that their normative/benchmark database is large enough to draw meaningful conclusions and that it covers the industries with which you would like to be compared. Trade associations and the Society for Human Resource Management also have databases of employee opinion surveys you can leverage. In many industries, such as health care, having normative data is often extremely valuable. The upside to normative/benchmark data is that it gives you numbers to aim for and provides a great way to set goals. The downside is that if you are ahead of the normative data, it could cause complacency, or if you are too far behind, it could demoralize your leaders. However, as we will discuss in a moment, catching up to or being ahead of your competitors on survey performance likely has no bearing on how your business is performing. Of greater value is discovering the attitudes or survey items that have the most significant impact on your organization's business outcomes — and focus on driving those.

Finally, the approach to reporting data across the organization is also something to consider. Most often, organizations will take a top-down approach, where senior leadership sees the overall survey results first and then local managers are provided with their results. This process has become much faster since most surveys are done electronically. However, the bottom-up or simultaneous approach can work just as well, where local managers and senior leaders receive their results at the same time. Again, it depends on your culture. No evidence suggests that one approach is more effective than another.

Taking Action

Applied research does tell us that giving feedback on the survey results and, most importantly, taking action on the results are critical ingredients to ensuring employees buy into action plans and participate in the next survey.[9] Digging deeper, the research suggests that you not only take action on the results but that you also communicate the fact that you are taking action. Many managers do take action on their survey results but neglect to make it clear that "I worked on this and fixed this because you asked me to on the survey." Make sure that your managers are not shy about communicating the actions they are taking are as a result of their interpretation of the survey results.

The Typical Approach to Employee Opinion Survey Execution

Our experiences have shown us that improving the approach organizations typically use to execute their employee opinion surveys is necessary. Often, organizations will not articulate the potential opportunity to drive business outcomes by surveying the workforce and will instead only focus on ill-defined outcomes such as engagement. We outline below the typical approach to employee survey implementation:

1. *Communicate the purpose of the survey.* This seems like a simple step, but do not underestimate its value. Senior leaders must actively communicate why the survey and the process are relevant to the organization and its employees. Communication cannot simply be "lip service." We recommend that the most senior leader, such as the CEO or president, communicate the launch of the survey. All employees need to understand that their feedback is valued and that leadership is committed to taking action based on their feedback.

2. *Conduct the employee survey.* Leaders will decide whether to conduct the survey in-house or outsource it to a survey vendor. The choice to conduct the survey in-house is often driven by cost concerns. The internal team or survey vendor will then launch the survey.

3. *Analyze the data and report results.* Typically, a lengthy report of all the items on the survey is generated for each leader. Leaders then may or may not share their

results with their team. Action plans are developed that focus on the low-scoring items and attempt to make improvements by searching out and implementing "best practices." For example, external vendors often provide action planning tools that include best practices for driving improvement on particular survey items.

Quite often, the organization will set an engagement index goal for every leader. The head of human resources may also implement some systemic goals or initiatives that are measured by how many employees participate. These metrics might even land on the organization's balanced scorecard; however, this is the closest the typical process comes to being business-focused.

4. *Survey again.* Usually 12 months later organizations start the process over again to determine whether any progress or improvement has been made.

These steps describe the typical survey process at both large and small organizations around the globe. Unfortunately, this approach limits the impact that the survey has on critical business outcomes. As a result, when the economy tightens, the employee survey is typically one of the first line items to be cut or delayed. By making the process business-focused, HR leaders can better demonstrate the value of surveying employees and ensure the sustainability of survey initiatives.

Building a Business-Focused Employee Survey

We will share examples from both UPS and Baptist Health Care to illuminate the process and reveal the critical steps to designing a business-focused survey. As a framework, here are the key steps in the business-focused approach:

1. Use a valid, reliable survey tool.
2. Conduct the survey annually.
3. Ensure that the survey results/goals are tracked on the organization's balanced scorecard.
4. Link the survey items to critical business outcomes and attitudes (e.g. turnover intentions).
5. Share the linkage analysis with senior and front-line leaders.
6. Make the results of the analysis simple and practical.
7. Conduct an ROI study to demonstrate the value of actions taken.

Use a Valid, Reliable Survey Instrument; Conduct the Survey Annually

Rather than go into a lengthy discussion about assessing the reliability and validity of your survey instrument — we will just hit the high notes. Assessing the reliability of the survey is vital, and many statistical approaches to doing this are available, but the most effective is called "internal reliability." This assessment is measured with "coefficient alpha," which is represented on a scale from 0 to 1.0. The key piece of information you need to know (or have your vendor show you) is that for your entire survey, and for the survey subcategories that you are measuring, the coefficient alpha must be at least 0.70. A coefficient alpha of 0.70 helps ensure that your results are reliable (i.e., useful for take-away assessment). Validity pertains directly to the question, "Do the items on my survey predict anything meaningful to my business?" To assess validity, you can use statistics to connect the survey subcategories or items to a relevant business outcome. If using an external vendor, require that it provide you with the validity studies for its survey instrument. Many significant decisions will be made using the survey data, so the survey tool you use must be both reliable and valid. (See Appendix B for an in-depth discussion of reliability and validity.)

In our experience, conducting the survey annually is the optimum frequency to maximize effectiveness. Attitudes take time to change, and initiatives take time to build, launch, and take hold, so surveying more frequently than every 12 months can place tremendous stress on the organization. Quite frankly, you will end up spending more time administering surveys than taking action on the results. However, shorter "pulse" surveys or a six-month survey cycle can be appropriate in certain situations.

Baptist Health Care in Pensacola, Florida, has been surveying and taking action on the results for years. The organization has won a Baldrige Award and has appeared on the *Fortune* list of best places to work for many years. The point is that Baptist Health Care has a strong culture, focused on employee engagement. For the organization, surveying every six months is both meaningful and practical. But most organizations should exercise caution in this regard because leaders can become enamored with *collecting data* and checking-in and not be as focused on *taking action* based on the results.

UPS has conducted its employee opinion survey annually since 1997 and has seen steady gains every year. Prior to 1997, the company conducted the survey twice a year and saw inconsistent results. This is only one example, but UPS is disciplined about its survey; it gets 90 percent participation in a union environment and is one of the most respected companies, in terms of management, in the world.

Ensure the Survey Results/Goals Are Tracked on the Organization's Balanced Scorecard

To get the focus of all leaders across the organization, the employee survey's quantitative outcome score (for example, level of commitment or satisfaction) should be tracked on the balanced scorecard. Indeed, many of the "best places to work" organizations track an employee survey metric.[10] This approach has both pros and cons to consider. The arguments in favor of adding survey results to the balanced scorecard follow:

- Leaders in the organization will focus on the treatment of people, and it will be on their agenda everyday of the week.
- Employees will realize that creating a strong work environment is an organizational priority and will take the annual survey and follow-up actions more seriously.

The argument opposing inclusion on the balanced scorecard is that the organization can become too focused on the acceptable "number." This emphasis can drive inappropriate behavior such as bribing employees with survey doughnuts and survey pizza, threatening employees with consequences if scores are not high in the department, or even attempting to keep less-than-happy employees from participating in the survey. We have seen it all, but these few arguments do not overcome the need for employee attitudes to be measured and tracked by the organization. Applied research we have conducted shows consistently that organizations that include their survey scores on a scorecard and that hold people accountable for those results have lower turnover and higher scores in the long run.

Link the Survey Items to Critical Business Outcomes and/or Important Attitudes

The Business Partner Roadmap™ provides a practical plan to build a business and/or commitment are not business outcomes; however, they can be drivers of business outcomes. To make your employee survey business-focused, link the data you collect to desirable business results (for example, employee or workgroup performance and turnover). As a reminder, the key questions to ask at each step in the Business Partner Roadmap™ are listed below:

1. *Determine critical outcomes.* On what outcomes/metrics are the senior leaders in this organization most focused?
2. *Create a cross-functional data team.* Who owns the specific data/metrics that senior leaders are focused on? How do I connect with those individuals to obtain the data?
3. *Assess outcome measures.* Are the primary business data/metrics collected at the appropriate level (for example, at department or district level) for me to make apples-to-apples comparisons?
4. *Analyze the data.* Do I have the statistical capabilities in-house, or do I need to look at a university or consulting firm to help me analyze the data?
5. *Build the program and execute.* Based on the linkage analysis, what is the highest priority/ROI project I should execute first?
6. *Measure and adjust.* How do I assess the change that has occurred and make adjustments to maximize effectiveness?

This process is straightforward, and it quickly allows you to align the results of the employee survey with business outcomes and demonstrate an impact on the organization's bottom line. This process is very time-sensitive, as organizations need to turn the survey data into meaningful action within a few weeks to two months (at a maximum) of the survey closing. The first three steps of this six-step process need to happen before the survey is even launched. Pulling together key stakeholder and key data is a time- and labor-intensive process and must be ready to go when the survey data are available. Step 4 (Analyze) should only take one to two weeks at a maximum, with communication of the analysis happening shortly thereafter. Step 5 (Building Programs) should be based purely on the analysis of the data and be completed within one to two months of the analysis (depending on the size and complexity of the program and initiatives needed). A case study will help to illuminate these points.

Survey Case Study: Baptist Health Care

We recently had the opportunity to help Baptist Health Care analyze its survey data to make it business-focused. As part of the process, we implemented the steps in the Business Partner RoadMap™. Leaders at Baptist Health Care were primarily focused on patient satisfaction, and were looking for additional approaches to positively impact their results. We took their survey data at the manager level and directly linked it to patient satisfaction results at the manager level. Specifically, we lined up the survey results for each manager with his or her year-to-date patient satisfaction scores. Having the patient satisfaction data at the manager level was necessary because we collected the employee survey data at that level.

Additionally, examining year-to-date patient satisfaction data was essential because it was the best barometer of performance on this metric and allowed us to look at cumulative performance in close proximity of time to the employee opinion survey data collection. We then analyzed the data using structural equation modeling (see Appendix for more detail on this methodology). The results of this analysis are presented in Figure 6.2.

Figure 6.2 shows us that Quality and Safety were the two survey categories that significantly drove patient satisfaction. Regarding Safety, when Baptist employees felt safe at work, literally in the building and walking to and from their cars in the parking lot, their ability to make patients feel satisfied increased. This outcome made sense because focusing on making patients feel cared for is difficult if you are uncomfortable in your surroundings. Additionally, not long before the survey was administered, the hospital had experienced a significant safety incident involving violence directed against hospital staff. All employees were aware of the incident, and it made the local news. The results thus helped to make an existing issue more of a priority to senior leaders. Scott Ginnetti, Director of People Development at Baptist, summed up the results:"This analysis allowed us to get senior team buy-in immediately on all of the safety initiatives that we had proposed. Tying the results to a business outcome that they all cared about took the urgency around safety to a new level."[11]

Figure 6.2

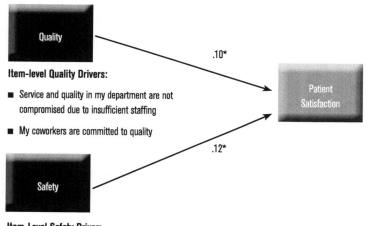

Item-level Quality Drivers:

- Service and quality in my department are not compromised due to insufficient staffing

- My coworkers are committed to quality

Item-Level Safety Driver:

- I feel safe at work (building, parking lot)

*Higher numbers indicate a stronger impact on patient satisfaction based on 0.0 – 1.0 scale.

While the senior leaders already understood the importance of the event and employee safety, the analysis directly linked safety to patient satisfaction — a key outcome metric for the organization. As a result of the linkage analysis, the sense of urgency on this topic was raised even higher. The analysis also allowed us to look at financial outcomes such as performance to budget and another compelling patient results metric "likelihood to recommend." This analysis uncovered additional drivers for the organization to work on at a systemic level and further allowed human resources to be viewed as a business partner at Baptist. Having the facts and data to support the improvement of a critical business outcome (patient satisfaction), and the ability to show the level of impact and specifically what to work on, is what creates those "seat at the table" opportunities for human resources.

Bringing Analytics to Front-line Leaders

One of the great advantages of applying analytics to people data is the ability to show business impact at a high level. However, turning that level and depth of insight into actionable information for leaders on the front lines is challenging. We have developed an approach/tool that will make your employee opinion survey more impactful. Our Strategic Survey HeatMap™ provides leaders with an easy-to-understand chart that summarizes their department or region's survey data into specific areas that prioritize action.

The Strategic Survey HeatMap™ was created after numerous clients expressed their frustrations with their survey vendors for providing them with huge amounts of data and lengthy reports. The HeatMap approach has been used before; however, the cause-effect analysis linking survey data to business outcomes and the inclusion of key drivers on the HeatMap (as we discuss in greater detail below) differentiates our approach. These clients further articulated that front-line leaders just did not have the time to pour over detailed results of 60 survey items with average scores, score distributions, benchmark scores, and colorful charts and then make informed decisions on strengths, weaknesses, and priorities for action. This input resonated with us. We empathized not only with HR leaders who were trying to create meaningful employee opinion surveys that could garner organizational buy-in but also with the front-line leaders who have a full plate every day of the week. The Strategic Survey HeatMap™ allows you to readily provide all leaders, at all levels, with a quick way of interpreting survey results and prioritizing exactly what they need to work on to drive business outcomes. According to Dennis Wade, Vice President of Human Resources at Baptist Health Care:

> Having the HeatMaps allows us to focus our entire leadership team on the factors that drive the outcomes that we want to achieve. The analytics bring a lot of credibility to the process and takes our survey from an assessment of attitudes to a discovery of new tools to impact our bottom line.[12]

A sample HeatMap is provided in Figure 6.3.

The Mechanics of the Strategic Survey HeatMap™

The first step in building the HeatMap is to work with senior leadership to identify the particular business outcome on which leaders wish to focus. For example, in Figure 6.3 the business outcome was delivery-driver productivity. By using the analytical techniques mentioned previously, we lined up each manager's employee opinion survey data with his or her year-to-date productivity data. The vertical axis on the HeatMap represents the percent favorable score achieved on each of the categories from the survey. The horizontal axis shows the level of impact that each of the survey categories had on the business outcome (driver productivity). The vertical bolded line near the middle of the HeatMap reveals the cutoff where the impact was significant or not significant. Every survey category to the right of the vertical bold line had a significant impact. Every survey category to the left of the vertical bold line did not have a significant impact.

The horizontal bold line represents the average "overall percent favorable goal" for the entire organization. This goal was determined by holding a meeting with senior leaders in the organization — it could have been set higher or lower; this all depends on your particular culture and needs. Any survey categories above the horizontal bold line are considered strengths. Any survey categories below the horizontal line are considered a developmental area.

The four quadrants of the HeatMap help leaders determine how to combine the level of impact and the level of strength of each survey category and to turn their results into an actionable plan.

Focus. The bottom right quadrant, the most important one, is labeled Focus. Any survey category that falls into this area is (1) scoring below the organizational average as measured by percent favorable and (2) a significant driver of productivity. In a nutshell, the two survey categories in the Focus bucket (Career Development and Management Communication, as noted in the legend) are essential, and this particular leader is not good at either of them. It thus makes sense that this particular leader put these two categories on her action plan. Front-line leaders love this approach because it reduces, perhaps substantially, their data analysis time and allows them to get down to business-focused plans quickly. Plus, when they realize that these are not just low scores but are also elements that are critical to a performance metric that directly impacts their bonus, front-line leaders buy in on both a personal and a business level. Human resources loves this approach because front-line leaders spend more time working on people issues that are driving the business.

Promote. The upper-right quadrant of the HeatMap is labeled Promote because these are the survey categories on which the leader is scoring well, and they are powerful drivers of business outcomes. For these survey categories, the leader

Figure 6.3 Sample of a Strategic Survey HeatMap™

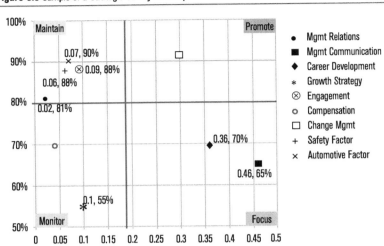

Career Development

Item	% Positive
I am comfortable discussing career opportunities at UPS with my immediate supervisor or manager	73
1 am provided the opportunity to develop valuable knowledge and skills by my immediate supervisor or manager.	67
My skill development is important to my immediate supervisor or manager.	70

Management Communications

Item	% Positive
I receive useful feedback from my immediate supervisor or manager	65
I feel comfortable discussing important workplace issues with my immediate supervisor or manager.	70
My immediate supervisor or manager is receptive to new ideas.	65
Different points of view are valued in my workgroup.	60

would want to highlight what she has been doing and the outcomes her people have achieved. This step will help keep her people focused on that particular area and ensure that they continue performing successfully.

Monitor. The bottom-left quadrant of the HeatMap is called Monitor because the survey categories that land here represent areas of weakness for this leader, but they are not highly significant to driving the productivity business outcome. Even so, this leader must still work on these areas regularly because they are weaknesses. The Focus areas are more crucial and should be taken care of first; however, monitoring these other areas will pay dividends.

Maintain. The top-left quadrant of the HeatMap is called Maintain — this represents the survey categories where this leader should just keep doing what she is doing. It shows the areas in which the leader is doing a great job, but these survey categories are not highly impactful on the productivity outcome. Maintaining her approach and intensity on these categories from the survey will keep paying off for this leader.

Bringing Analytics to Mid-Level Managers

At Baptist Health Care, we have taken the process an additional step and created HeatMaps for each hospital leader so that the organization can hold individual workgroup managers accountable for survey results that drive the business (see Table 6.1). At this level, the hospital leader can quickly see how each department scored on the different survey categories, while paying special attention to the first four categories (retention, mission/goals, commitment, and senior leadership) because these were shown to have a significant impact on a critical business outcome — patient satisfaction.

Creating HeatMaps for each hospital leader gives a quick and practical look at performance results on the employee survey. Additionally, the HeatMap consolidates an overwhelming amount of data into a practical format that managers can easily use to drive action and accountability.

Calculating ROI

As with all capital investments, demonstrating a return on investment is a must to obtain budget for large projects. Unfortunately, human resources has a somewhat inconsistent track record in this area. In the HeatMap example, we talked about the impact of management communications and career development on productivity. Figure 6.4 shows the quantifiable impact from this analysis.

Table 6.1

Department Name	HOSPITAL A KEY PERFORMANCE DRIVERS			
	Retention	Mission/Goals	Commitment	Sr. Leadership
5610 PATIENT FINANCIAL SERVICES	67%	67%	71%	75%
4627 OUTPATIENT CLINIC	67%	93%	100%	53%
3300 EMERGENCY ROOM	69%	80%	84%	69%
3101 MED/SURG HALL	71%	91%	90%	83%
4620 PHYSICAL THERAPY	75%	100%	100%	83%
4100 LABORATORY	77%	93%	88%	86%
5600 NURSING ADMINISTRATION	80%	97%	90%	87%
4206 RADIOLOGY	83%	94%	93%	93%
3200 OPERATING ROOM	83%	95%	94%	86%
5000 FOOD SERVICES	85%	100%	98%	100%
3112 ICCU	88%	96%	97%	96%
4304 RESPIRATORY THERAPY	96%	98%	100%	100%
5023 MAT MGMT	100%	100%	100%	100%
5602 EMPLOYEE HEALTH	100%	100%	100%	100%
5602 EMPLOYEE HEALTH	100%	80%	98%	70%

Leadership	Corp Image	Co-Workers	Recognition	Safety	Benefits	Compensation
43%	73%	72%	29%	58%	63%	29%
80%	60%	90%	80%	100%	75%	33%
86%	70%	84%	64%	69%	50%	48%
90%	88%	93%	81%	91%	84%	58%
69%	95%	100%	58%	100%	88%	92%
94%	88%	81%	82%	87%	77%	23%
88%	100%	95%	93%	93%	75%	27%
84%	87%	91%	79%	98%	89%	76%
94%	92%	92%	100%	95%	82%	79%
96%	97%	96%	95%	100%	93%	79%
90%	85%	100%	67%	92%	64%	50%
97%	100%	100%	93%	96%	83%	93%
100%	100%	81%	83%	100%	100%	75%
100%	100%	100%	100%	100%	100%	80%
90%	82%	98%	70%	90%	15%	30%

Figure 6.4

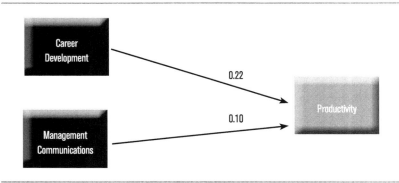

As evidenced in the figure, the impact of employees' perceptions of career development on productivity has a value of 0.22. That is, a one full-point gain in career development perceptions would be associated with a significant 0.22 gain in the productivity metric. This also means, for example, that a one-half point gain in career development perceptions would be associated with a 0.11 gain in the productivity metric. If a full-point gain on the productivity metric meant $2 million dollars to this organization, then the ROI of gaining a full point on career development perceptions would be $440,000. We calculated this number by multiplying 0.22 by $2 million. Such ROI calculations help HR leaders demonstrate the value of employee surveys to the business and become true business partners.

Practical Tips

- *Expect and request that your survey vendor provide validity studies for their instrument.* The instrument you use in your organization must be valid, reliable, and predictive of important outcomes. If it is not, you run a high risk of making poor decisions or investments based on erroneous survey data.
- *The employee opinion survey strategy should focus on driving business outcomes.* Employee engagement or satisfaction is *not* a business outcome. It never has been. Put the focus on outcomes that actually matter to the organization — such as retention, customer satisfaction, or productivity.
- *Make the results practical and action-oriented.* Although the statistical analysis processes we describe are best suited for a textbook, the results they generate are clear, strategic, actionable, and have a clear ROI.

■ *Gather outcome data from key stakeholders early in the process.* This step can be a process in itself, just to get the right data in the right place at the right level at the right time. Reach out cross-functionally ahead of time so that you can turn around your analyses, HeatMaps, and recommendations promptly at the conclusion of the survey.

■ *Demonstrate the business linkage analysis to all levels.* Often the linkage analysis (if done at all) is relegated to the boardroom for review with senior leaders. While this is a great place to get started, the execution takes place on the front lines. So get the word out about how attitudes drive business results. The Strategic Survey HeatMaps™ are a focused and relevant way to show each leader exactly what they should work on to drive critical business results.

■ *Link engagement data to more than one business outcome, if possible.* As you know, not all leaders in your organization are focused on the same business outcome. So incorporate local, relevant business outcomes into your HeatMaps and senior level presentations so that you get buy-in across the organization. For example, although a productivity metric may be strong in operations, the focus in corporate IT maybe on retention. Provide each function with the data and analysis around outcomes that are most relevant to them — doing so will continue to increase your stature as a business partner.

CHAPTER 7

Employee Training

Training has become a catch-all word in many organizations to mean just about anything associated with learning or development. Most organizations hold an intuitive belief that training is a good thing, so more of it must be better.[1] For example, General Electric typically comments on how much it invests every year in training for their employees (over $1 billion), and they have quite a reputation for building leaders. In this chapter, we will review the research that provides practical advice around learning principles, training design, and evaluation for individual courses. We will then focus on how to build a business-focused training strategy — an area that the research has generally overlooked — using facts and data that link employee training to your overall business strategy.

What the Research Tells Us

Generally, employee training refers to the processes by which individuals acquire job-related skills.[2] Training involves the transfer of particular knowledge or skills from an expert to a learner in an attempt to improve job performance. Formal training is one component of employee development and, when appropriately integrated with other developmental experiences (for example, leadership development, coaching/mentoring, and experience-based learning), is generally considered an effective means of improving employee performance and preparing employees for future roles in the organization.

Principles of Adult Learning

Prior to designing and implementing employee training, having a foundational understanding of the way in which adults (for our purposes, age 18 and older) learn in the workplace is essential. Adult learning principles are the building blocks of the employee learning process and can be applied to both formal and informal training initiatives. Researchers have described adult learning as a process of self-directed inquiry. Several key factors that distinguish adult learners can help guide you in developing effective training programs for this population:

- *Self-direction.* Adult learners are autonomous and prefer to have some control over the nature, timing, and direction of the learning process.
- *Experience.* Adult learners have accumulated workplace experiences and knowledge that serve as a resource for learning.
- *Readiness to learn.* Adult learners tend to be goal-oriented; they are ready to develop the skills and abilities pertinent to their role.
- *Relevance-oriented.* Adult learners are oriented toward relevant, problem-focused learning that may immediately be applied.
- *Motivation to learn.* Adult learners are internally motivated to pursue new knowledge and are most motivated to learn when the need to know the information is clear (that is, when the relevance or application of new information is obvious).
- *Cooperative learning.* Adult learners are most receptive to learning in cooperative environments characterized by mutual trust and shared expectations.[3]

Learning Strategies

In addition to the principles of adult learning, trainers/educators can utilize a variety of specific strategies to enhance learning outcomes. These strategies include practice, whole-versus-partial learning, utilizing advanced organizers, and providing feedback.

Practice, one of the most fundamental learning strategies, occurs when trainees learn something new and are provided with an opportunity to demonstrate the newly acquired knowledge or skill during training. Adults are more likely to retain knowledge and transfer new skills to the work environment when they actively participate in the learning process (i.e., practice new skills during the training session), as opposed to receiving new information passively.

Researchers have identified several key aspects of practice that can influence the way in which learning happens and, more importantly, how what is learned is transferred to the job.

- *Over learning.* This aspect of practice refers to practicing a task more than is necessary for the new knowledge or skills to transfer back to the job. In general, trainers encourage over learning when tasks need to be performed almost without thinking. For example, police officers may over learn how to draw their weapon so that the process becomes automatic when they encounter a dangerous situation in the field.
- *Massed versus distributed practice.* This type of practice refers to the frequency and duration of practice during training sessions. Massed practice entails practicing for an extended period of time without taking breaks. Distributed practice involves taking breaks between practice sessions and is almost always

preferred by trainees to massed practice in order to enhance the retention and transfer of new knowledge and skills.

- *Fidelity.* This aspect refers to how similar the training context is to the actual job environment. For example, cashier training for a retail store would be considered high fidelity if the trainees were trained on an actual cash register with "fake" customers rather than role-playing during training without customers or a cash register.[4]

In addition to practice, other learning strategies include organizing learning into wholes versus parts, utilizing advanced organizers, and providing feedback.

- *Whole-learning* occurs when trainees learn an entire task or concept at one time.
- *Partial-learning* involves breaking a task or concept into several, manageable pieces. In general, partial-learning has been found to be more effective for more complex tasks because it reduces the chances of overloading trainees.
- *Advanced organizers* entails using charts, graphs, pictures, or mnemonic; advanced organizers help reduce the chance of overloading trainees because they organize new information using familiar objects or memorable devices.
- *Accurate and timely feedback* is an essential part of the learning process — trainees will learn more effectively when given an opportunity to make mistakes, receive feedback, and correct their mistakes.

Learning Outcomes

Employee training is a means of conveying valuable information regarding the skills and knowledge critical to employees' on-the-job performance. Although training often happens in a classroom, training outcomes are rarely realized until trainees apply their new learning in real-life work situations. Training outcomes have been broadly categorized into the following three buckets:

- *Cognitively-based learning* refers to acquiring job-relevant facts or conceptual knowledge. For example, bank tellers may memorize their bank's savings and loans options and the pros and cons of each so that they can readily share this information with customers.
- *Skill-based learning* refers to acquiring the technical or motor skills necessary to perform the job. For example, an employee working on an assembly line may learn how to operate machinery in a safe and efficient manner, or office workers may learn how to use computer software that is relevant to their job.
- *Affective learning* refers to generating beliefs or emotional attachments that will motivate an employee to act in a certain way. Training new employees to value the company's product or mission and to perform their job responsibilities in a

manner consistent with the company's standards of performance are examples of affective learning.

Effective Design and Execution

Training design refers to the way in which objectives and learning principles are used in the training program, as well as the instructional strategies used in the delivery of the training to achieve the stated goals. A well-designed training program begins with the following characteristics:

- *Clearly stated objectives.* Specifies the knowledge, skills, or attitudes (KSAs) that trainees are to develop as a result of the training program. Training objectives help trainers decide how best to structure the program and help students acquire the desired knowledge, skills, and abilities more successfully. Objectives are specific and measurable. They define what the learner should be able to do as a result of the training and at what level of competence. Once the objectives have been established, appropriate learning principles and strategies may be incorporated into the training program to maximize learning outcomes and help ensure transfer of training.

- *Carefully considered format.* New technologies, like web-based delivery, have transformed the training landscape, reducing administration costs and helping make training more accessible to telecommuters, expatriates, and remote workers. However, some have questioned the effectiveness of such methods. In a recent large-scale study, researchers found that when accounting for a lack of or reduced features, such as amount of trainer-trainee interaction and feedback, any benefits of web-based training disappear.[5]

Measurement and Evaluation

The goals of training should be not only to provide new information but to make sure that the information is applied back at the participant's job. Researchers call this process "transfer of training," and it is the most critical outcome of any training program. If new KSAs do not transfer beyond the training venue, then the time and resources spent on training are wasted (resulting in a poor ROI).

Prior to implementing a new training program, determine how the program will be evaluated. Ideally, training should be evaluated along more than one dimension. Training programs can be evaluated using Donald L. Kirkpatrick's evaluation criteria, which are organized into the following four levels:

- *Reactions* are the most basic level and focus on participants' perceptions of the effectiveness of the training. Evaluating reactions beyond making minor tweaks in how the content is delivered is of little value.

- *Learning* is an evaluation of the extent to which new KSAs were learned by the trainee. The most thorough way to assess learning is to evaluate trainees' knowledge and skills prior to the training and again upon conclusion of the training. Called a pre-test, post-test approach, it is a relatively rigorous assessment of the learning that occurred as a result of the training.

- *Transfer* refers to the application of training content back at the trainee's job. To assess transfer, an option is to implement multi-rater (360-degree) assessments of the trainee upon completion of the training. Such assessments provide a holistic perspective of the extent to which trainees have transferred new knowledge and skills to their work role.

- *Results* are about the impact of the training on bottom-line organizational outcomes (e.g., improved performance or increased revenue). As discussed in Chapter 1, linkage analysis is the approach most effective here. However, such analyses often elude HR leaders and are rarely used in organizations — to the detriment of the training department and HR's credibility.[6]

Outside Influences Impacting Outcomes

When contemplating how best to design a training program and measure its effectiveness, it is necessary to consider the effects of individual and organizational characteristics. Researchers have found numerous aspects of individuals and organizations that can influence the level of impact/transfer of training.

Individual characteristics. Various individual differences, such as cognitive ability and personality, can influence training outcomes. Similarly, the extent to which learners are motivated and believe in their ability to acquire and transfer new knowledge (i.e., learning self-efficacy) can alter the effectiveness of training.[7] Although some individual differences may be present prior to training and are relatively enduring throughout training (e.g., personality), others may develop or change throughout the training process (such as motivation or self-efficacy). For instance, motivated learners will likely become unmotivated if the training is irrelevant or does not capture their attention. Likewise, confident learners could experience a decrease in self-efficacy if the training is unexpectedly challenging.

Another individual characteristic that has been found to affect transfer of training is the trainee's goal orientation.[8] Goal orientation refers to an individual's predisposition to pursue either learning outcomes or performance outcomes in achievement settings. Individuals with a learning goal orientation are motivated to increase their competence and to excel at challenging tasks. In contrast, individuals with a performance goal orientation are motivated to prove their ability to others and to avoid situations in which they may fail or be perceived as incompetent. Researchers have found that individuals with learning goal orientations are more likely to experience long-term transfer of training than individuals with performance goal orientation.[9]

Organization characteristics. Characteristics of the organization can also affect training outcomes. In particular, transfer of training is likely to be affected by the extent to which the organization as a whole and the learner's manager in particular support the training initiative. Training outcomes will likely be limited if supervisors do not view the training as valuable and support trainees in using their newly learned skills and knowledge back on the job. Similarly, executive level leaders should demonstrate support of training through communications and by attending training themselves. Finally, job constraints such as a lack of flexibility, limited freedom to integrate new learning on the job, and insufficient resources to carry out new skills at work may interfere with training effectiveness. For example, imagine going to a new software class and returning to work to find the old software still in use.

The next section explains how to create a training strategy that is business-focused and driven directly by the business strategy.

Building a Business-Focused Training Strategy

The research on employee training comes up short in two key areas. The first is in how to create a comprehensive training strategy that is connected to the business strategy via organizational capabilities and competencies. And the second is demonstrating the cause-and-effect relationships between training and business outcomes and using this information to guide training investment decisions.

Creating an Aligned Training Strategy

Many consultants and practitioners will build a business case for their training curriculum around it being "aligned" to the business strategy. Oftentimes this alignment happens when the business strategy points to a need to be "innovative," for example, and the consultant or practitioner has an "innovation training" product. On the surface this appears to achieve business strategy alignment; however, having the right title for the program does not mean that alignment has been achieved.

True alignment comes not only when the training is linked to the business strategy but also when the connection between training curricula and business strategy has been made through a rigorous set of competencies that were creat-ed based on overall organizational capabilities. Figure 7.1 reveals the overarching process.

Figure 7.1

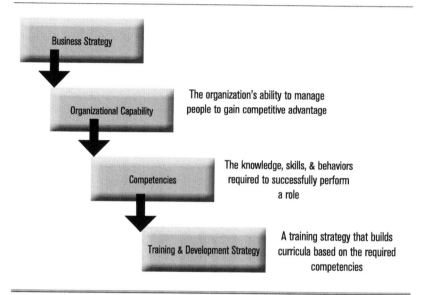

Remember that aligning a training program with a big, overarching business theme or topic will not lead to measurable results. The link between the training strategy and organizational capability can only come about when the capabilities are broken down into their core competencies. Figure 7.2 provides an overview of the contributions that capabilities, competencies, and training strategy make to the organizational strategy and how these components fit together.

Figure 7.2

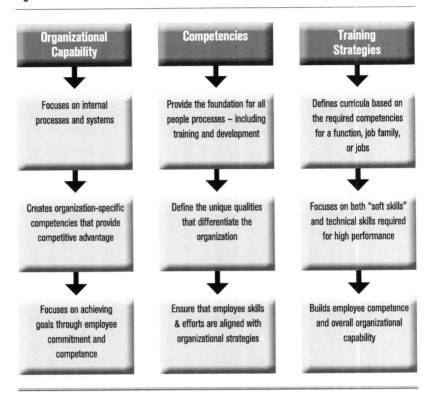

Creating a training strategy either in a vacuum or by simply taking a look at your organization's strategic plan will likely yield limited positive results. Instead, your training strategy should be developed to address the specific core competencies that the organization has identified. Another key tenet of building a training strategy is to use analytics to uncover which competencies or training programs are actually driving business outcomes. Although we discussed this linkage process more thoroughly in Chapter 1, we briefly discuss below two ways to make your training strategy more business-focused and to calculate a direct return on investment.

■ *Analyze competency data to uncover the specific competencies that drive business outcomes in various departments across the organization, and then focus on training programs that target these competencies.* Whether you have collected competency ratings from a multi-rater assessment or through your performance management system, the objective is to line up the competency performance data with relevant business outcomes for each individual. Breaking these analyses out by department is also appropriate, for example, by linking the sales department's competencies to sales performance data. We conducted this type of analysis with the sales function of a medium-sized pharmaceutical company with its multi-rater assessment data. We linked the competency ratings on the sales function's multi-rater assessment to individual market share performance results. The competencies that had the largest cause-effect relationship with the market share business outcome became the most critical components of the company's training strategy. This focused training strategy resulted in higher levels of sales representative performance, with the sales department outperforming its sales goal.

As this example demonstrates, designing your training strategy around competencies that drive business outcomes helps you to build a straightforward business case and calculate the expected return on investment for the training. The return on investment is calculated by using a statistical indicator called a beta weight that demonstrates the impact of the competency on the business outcome. The beta weight can range from zero to 1.00. A beta weight of 0.25 means that for every full point that you increase competency performance, you will see a 0.25 improvement in the business outcome. If the business outcome increases by $1 million, your impact would be $250,000. If you spent $100,000 on the training courses, your ROI would be 250 percent (250,000/100,000).

■ *Analyze current training data (participation and skill/knowledge acquisition) to uncover which current training courses have a significant impact on business outcomes.* The second business-focused approach to building out your training strategy and corresponding business case is to conduct a similar linkage analysis using current training program data. The ultimate outcome of any training program is to be able to confidently say that it had the impact it was supposed to have on a specific business outcome. The two most effective approaches to take in linking training data and business data are:

» Connecting training participation rates to business outcome data
» Connecting training performance data to business outcome data

We worked with a retail organization looking to uncover key people drivers of a business issue called product shrink (i.e., the loss of product due to employee theft or "too much time on shelf"). Through the HRIS platform and learning management system, organization leaders were able to provide us with data on completion rates for training courses at each of their stores and with performance data (i.e. test scores) for those training courses. We utilized a statistical approach called structural equation modeling (see Chapter 1 for details) and discovered that participation in particular training courses had a significant impact on product shrink. As a result of this analysis, the training department was able to tailor its strategy around enhancing participation in these two specific courses. More importantly, it was able to demonstrate a return on investment for these courses, in the form of reduced product shrink. See Figure 7.3 for the ROI calculation.

Figure 7.3 Product Shrink ROI Calculation

- Current State: $93 million in annualized shrink

- Goal: Increase Ethics Course participation from 65 percent to 95 percent
  - » 95 percent participation could result in additional savings of $4.3 million
  - » Approximate cost of increasing training participation is $1,100,000
  - » Expected ROI: 390 percent

Intervention	Beta	Potential Shrink Impact	Level of Investment
Ethics Course	0.10	$4.3 million	Under-investing
Shrink Course	0.09	$8.4 million	Under-investing

These two approaches will help guide your decision-making and allow you to invest in training initiatives that will have the greatest impact on the business. As the organization views the connection between business strategy and capabilities/ competencies, it will look to the training function to meet its needs in building out the competencies. This is a perfect opportunity to catalog your training curricula by competency, which will uncover the gaps in the training curricula and allow you to be proactive in filling those gaps. Once you have strong competencies on which to base your training, creating specific, customized courses that meet the exact needs of the organization becomes much more straightforward, whether you build the courses internally or externally.

Leveraging existing curricula that focus on the key competencies of interest is often possible; however, developing new curricula to effectively address each of the core competencies may be necessary. Additionally, as the business strategy changes, the capabilities critical to achieving that strategy will also change. This situation will obviously require a refinement of the competency model and associated training strategy.

Practical Tips

- Align your initial training strategy to the defined competencies and capabilities of the organization.
- Capture competency ratings data (via multi-rater assessment, for example) as well as training participation and performance data for every course possible.
- Statistically link training participation data to business outcomes (group outcomes or individual outcomes) to show the impact of training on the bottom line.
- Craft a refined training strategy based on the statistical analysis of both competency and training performance data.

- Calculate ROI on a regular basis to show the continuing business impact of your training strategy.
- Measure the effectiveness of your training strategy regularly and use the data to refine your strategy, as needed.

CHAPTER 8

Career Development

Many organizations struggle to clearly define and support the career development of their employees. As organizations have become flatter and career pathing has become more versatile and less structured, the roles of the organization and the employee in career development have changed. As a result, a significant need exists in organizations and HR departments for a more comprehensive process to support the career growth of employees.

Another major factor that has "muddied the waters" of career development in recent history is that the meaning of "career" has shifted from a lifetime spent in a single organization to collective professional experiences across multiple organizations. This change occurred when the idea of "lifetime" employment died in the 1990s.[1] The official end of this era was signified by the massive layoffs that occurred in the United States in the 1990s, with the most prominent example being IBM's first official downsizing. Prior to this event, "Big Blue" embodied the idea that an employee could sustain long-term career growth, assuming solid job performance, within a single organization.

Today, the norm is moving from employer to employer, often with significant changes in one's chosen career. For younger Baby Boomers and most Generation Xers, the idea of staying at one organization for an entire career seems archaic, if not ridiculous. Recent statistics collectively report that the average Generation Y employee remains in a job for 3.3 years and a Generation X employee for 3.8 years — even Baby Boomers are only averaging about eight years.[2] Even though career development typically spans multiple employers, organizations still play a role in helping employees progress in their career.

In addition to the changing view of a career, employees' needs and values have changed. In today's organization, the focus has shifted toward helping employees acquire valuable, transferable skills, thus motivating them to perform at high levels and positioning organizations to remain competitive in their marketplace. To help HR departments address these changing needs, this chapter will review career development research and literature, define a framework and process for career development, and provide a case study that reveals an application of this process within an organization.

What the Research Tells Us

Career development is defined as a combination of enrichment activities (i.e., mentoring, performance feedback, training, and coaching) directed at assisting employees in attaining career goals.[3] Before we invest time and resources in addressing career development, an organization must understand the business case for implementing career-focused initiatives or programs. Participation in career development programs has been shown to increase employee productivity and commitment and to reduce employee turnover, thus contributing to succession planning efforts. Additionally, career development programs have been found to positively impact organizational innovation and change initiatives.[4] Our research in organizational settings has shown that strong career development programs increase retention of high performers, improve perceptions of a strong future with the organization, and enhance employee commitment. Finally, well-structured career development initiatives can help organizations attract future talent and remain competitive in their marketplace.

- *Talent attracts talent.* Being perceived as an organization that attracts and develops top talent is a valued commodity. Companies known for hiring and retaining the highest-caliber employees and helping their employees grow professionally will generate an attractive reputation and be perceived as a desirable place for top talent to work.

- *Competitive advantage.* Most leaders assume that their employees are their "most valuable asset." This notion has even more credence in a service-based economy, where service delivery, innovation, and, ultimately, financial success are linked directly to the performance of employees. Although HR departments often struggle to quantify the impact of employees on the bottom line, the assumption that employees matter is generally held to be true by most senior leaders within organizations.[5]

Based on existing research, growing and developing talent to help retain valuable employees and maximize the return-on-hiring investments makes sense for organizations. However, as a central theme of this book, we recommend quantifying the impact of career development programs on key business outcomes *within the context of your organization* and not simply assume that the link exists.

Environmental Factors Influencing Career Development

Prior to the 1990s, a consistent model of career development held true. Traditional career development theory focused on the significant roles and stages of career development that occur throughout a person's life. These theories focused on the interaction between life events and individual characteristics that influenced an employee's decision-making and career choices. Researchers defined different life stages (for example, early life and mid-life) and studied the impact of life stages on career choices and the employee's expressed needs/desires regarding his/her career.[6] These life stages influenced employees' career expectations, which ultimately defined their expectations of their employer — oftentimes the same employer for their entire career.

Over time, the relationship between employees and employers has evolved such that employees have become increasingly independent, and their careers frequently traverse multiple organizations. Only until recently, a job candidate's resume that depicted multiple company changes was viewed negatively. "Job hopping" was frowned upon. Today, such cross-organizational job mobility is the norm.[7] Hiring managers are now looking for increases in responsibility, role progression, or new skill development, irrespective of whether such growth has occurred within one organization or across multiple organizations. This change has altered how employers and employees view career development. In addition, the following environmental factors have changed the way in which careers are managed:

- Organizations are flatter, providing fewer opportunities for vertical promotions (for example, from office manager to regional manager); therefore, career development can no longer focus exclusively on achieving vertical promotions or on ascending the organizational ranks.

- Adults are having children later in life — during the prime years of their careers. This reality, coupled with greater expectations regarding work/life flexibility (to be discussed in Chapter 11), shifts the traditional notion of career development away from simply moving up the ladder (e.g., increasing salary or obtaining promotions) toward moving into positions that afford the balance and flexibility that employees seek. Additionally, many employees are taking care of their parents during the prime years of their careers, which places greater demands on employees and further increases the value of work/life balance.

- Fewer "lifetime" employment expectations, particularly as the younger generations enter the workforce, change the notions of organizational commitment and loyalty and have contributed to some employers' hesitation to invest in the development of their employees.

- Increased life expectancy — which means people are working longer. The U.S. Bureau of Labor Statistics in July reported that the 65-plus workforce increased more than 101 percent between 1977 and 2007.[8]

- As technology changes quickly and our economy has become more global with increased competition, skills become obsolete more quickly. Technology-related skills may have a shelf life as short as four years.

- When the economy is down, keeping a focus on career development programs, particularly for high-performers, is critical, as they will likely be the first to leave when the economy turns around, especially if they were forgotten about during the downturn.[9]

Job hopping and changing environmental conditions present something of a Catch-22 for HR leaders — should they be wary of job hoppers and try to hire individuals who show longevity in their work history, or should they create a strong culture of career development so that the pipeline is always full of internal and external candidates? In response to such novel challenges, companies have begun to approach career development as more of a partnership with employees. This trend means that organizations work with employees to assess their career aspirations, identify existing business needs, and look for synergies between the two in an effort to align career development plans with the business needs and goals of the organization. Specifically, the career partnership approach aligns employees' career goals with the needs of the organization and involves interventions that augment employees' existing skills and abilities while helping to fill organizational competency gaps.[10] This model consists of two dimensions: career planning and career management. Career planning is focused on identifying employees' abilities, interests, career goals, and development needs. Career management, on the other hand, is focused on identifying the organization's career development strategy and future staffing needs. Organizations that are successful at integrating both the individual and organization's needs are better equipped to meet new demands and to match qualified employees with unexpected company needs.

As a result of this partnership model, career development programs have become much more self-directed and involve opportunities that are naturally embedded in employees' work context. In addition, the move toward career development as a partnership between organizations and employees has resulted in the following changes to organizations' career development strategies:[11]

- Many organizations now focus more heavily on creating career development paths that allow employees to progress naturally in their career while acquiring knowledge, skills, and abilities (KSAs) and achieving career development milestones. These development paths have evolved from linear to multidirectional, providing employees with more cross-functional skills and opportunities in various departments. For example, job rotations or assignments that afford employees the opportunity to gain experience in a novel functional area have become increasingly popular.

- Organizations have developed methods to assess the readiness of employees to take on increased responsibility. For example, organizations often use multi-rater

(360-degree) performance assessments (see Chapter 5) to assess employees' readiness for new roles. Premature movement not only impacts the performance of the individual and the organization but can also lead to increased turnover.

- HR professionals have become increasingly attentive to potential fairness issues. For example, fairness issues can arise when employees perceive career development initiatives, or promotions, as only targeting specific groups. The provision of defined career paths for each of the roles in the organization helps improve perceptions of fairness. These paths elucidate for employees what KSAs and experiences are needed to be considered for a certain role. The use of valid assessment tools, such as performance appraisals, also adds additional objective measurement to the career/promotion process and enhances perceptions of fairness. The potential for litigation exists in this area, so the more objective your process, the less risk you will incur.

- Communication of development and training opportunities has become increasingly crucial to the success of career development programs. Communication plays a distinctive role in perceptions of fairness and equity around development opportunities. Open discussion and "posting" of opportunities for employees should occur versus what can be perceived as back-room maneuvering for jobs (or jobs that were "filled" before they were officially open).

- Managers have begun to play an increasingly vital role in employees' career development, as their support (or lack thereof) significantly impacts employees' career motivation and mobility.

- Employees' perceptions of various aspects of their work environment (as assessed with employee opinion surveys), such as supervisor and team support, recognition, and effective feedback, can influence the career development process. In our research within organizations, we have discovered that employees who perceive higher levels of effective supervisor feedback and recognition show stronger commitment to the organization and perceive greater opportunities for career development.

- Organizations have begun to reconsider the effects of generational differences on career attitudes and expectations. While much of the recent career development research has focused on generational differences, many of the differences found within generational groups can be explained by individual differences and career stages. In a groundbreaking study, the authors found only negligible generational differences in employees' learning preferences, desire to gain "hard" or "soft" skills, and overall beliefs in development at work. HR leaders tend to place employees into categories based on their age or generational cohort. However, this approach may be shortsighted, as career development is truly about the individual (their values, interests, competencies, and goals) — and that is where the focus should be. Therefore, organizations should focus less on generational groups and more on career stages and individual needs and goals.[12]

Building a Business-Focused Career Development Process

Before building a new career development process or revisiting an existing one, HR leaders must first build the business case. The Business Partner Roadmap™ (as described in Chapter 1) provides an overview of the steps HR leaders should take to build the business case for career development initiatives and to identify the goals of their career development process.

The most common method for justifying the investment in employees' careers is to link employee attitudes about career development opportunities with turnover or turnover intentions (for example, with responses to the question "*How long do you plan to stay at this organization?*" on an employee survey). Most employee surveys include a few items focused on career development, such as items regarding employees' perceptions of the availability and quality of training opportunities and their beliefs that the organization or organizational leaders support ongoing

Figure 8.1

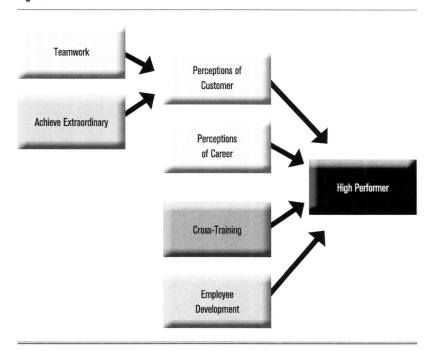

development. Employee survey data is generally easy to obtain and can readily be statistically linked to turnover or turnover intentions. The results of the linkage analysis (assuming they are significant) allow HR leaders to objectively connect employees' career development perceptions to a meaningful business outcome (e.g., turnover or the estimated cost of turnover), thereby creating a strong business case for investment in career development initiatives. The business case will help HR leaders gain the support of and critical resources from senior and front-line leaders.

The ways to effectively show the return on investment (ROI) for career development programs are numerous. First, linking career development attitudes (on an employee opinion survey) to turnover and productivity numbers for both individuals and workgroups across the organization will demonstrate value. Second, tracking high potentials and high performers and demonstrating a reduction in turnover levels among these populations as a result of career development initiatives will also show ROI. For example, we helped a large service organization understand why their high performers were leaving the organization at an undesirable rate. Using the analytic processes discussed throughout this book and focusing on such factors as high performers' competencies, attitudes, training, experiences, and opportunities, we uncovered the drivers of high-performer turnover depicted in Figure 8.1 on the previous page.

As evidenced in the figure, perceptions of career development were one of the critical drivers of high-performer turnover. Specifically, high performers who perceived few career development opportunities were more likely to leave the organization. We used this analysis to create a compelling business case that prompted senior leaders to buy in to the idea of improving career development. The analysis also created a sustained focus on building programs to cross-train all employees, with an emphasis on high-performing/high-potential employees. Rather than guessing at what drove high performers to leave or relying on unreliable exit interviews — the data and analysis told the true story.

Effective Execution

Once the business case has been established, the next step is to build and deploy the process/program. We outline below a basic framework for creating a customized career development solution. This approach assumes that the career development solution is being deployed in today's typical work environment — where the employee is the primary owner of his or her career development. Furthermore, it is meant to be applied to the entire employee population, not a subset of high potentials. These more specialized approaches are described in the leadership development and succession planning chapters.

Defining Roles in the Career Development Process

The first step in building the process is to clearly define roles and expectations for the organization, managers, and employees. Table 8.1 provides a description of accountabilities that can be customized to meet your specific organizational culture and business needs.

Table 8.1 is meant to be a starting point in defining the roles that each stakeholder might play in the career development process. Customizing these roles to your organization's culture is important. For some cultures, the employee's role may be more pronounced, while in others it may be the manager who is highly active in the employee's career development. However, these roles should be expressly delineated and communicated upfront to clarify expectations surrounding the career development process. Setting the tone and expectations for managers and employees is critical to the success of any business process. Even in today's self-directed environment, we are still surprised at how many employees sit around waiting for the organization or manager to "develop" their career. By simply stating what may seem obvious, employees and managers will be empowered to fulfill their respective roles in the process.

Table 8.1

Stakeholder	Career Development Accountabilities
Organization	■ Educate employees about their career management responsibilities
	■ Provide a process and tools to help employees manage their careers
	■ Educate managers on their career management coaching responsibilities
	■ Provide fair and equal job access to employees
	■ Encourage and support retention of employees within the organization
Manager	■ Clarify the organization's strategic direction and relate an individual's career goals to the organization's needs
	■ Ensure that each employee has a career development plan
	■ Provide guidance and coaching around career development
	■ Provide honest, insightful feedback to employees regarding their career opportunities and performance
	■ Help employees identify developmental assignments and activities
Employee	■ Increase self-awareness of competencies, experiences, interests, and opportunities
	■ Seek feedback and career advice
	■ Develop skills and competencies needed to accomplish career goals
	■ Develop a career plan and execute

Defining the Career Development Process

The next step is to define a self-directed process that allows employees to take ownership of their careers. Again, the process appears simple; however, being explicit will reduce confusion and provide employees and managers with the necessary tools and knowledge to execute the process effectively. The steps for employees to follow in the self-directed career development process are discussed next.

Become more self-aware and establish a direction for managing your career. Many factors, including personal preferences, values, experiences, and aspirations, influence employees' choices about their careers. A self-assessment of these preferences serves as the foundation for an employees' self-directed career development process. Employees need to be provided with a framework and assessment tools to guide them in their self-directed career exploration. To this end, we have developed a successful framework called Career ADVICE™. The acronym ADVICE stands for Assess and Develop with Values, Interests, Competencies, and Experiences. Within this framework, employees will examine the following:

- What they value in a job (i.e., their likes and dislikes or aspirations)
- Their existing strengths and opportunities for improvement
- The significant, job-relevant experiences they have had (e.g., functional experiences, management/leadership experiences, subject matter expertise, and technical experience)
- The alignment between their development needs and opportunities available through the organization

An overview of our Career ADVICE™ framework is depicted in Table 8.2.

This table represents the complexity of making career choices and illustrates why self-awareness is fundamental to the career development process. Employees should consider both individual and organizational factors as they make career decisions. The first four questions in the self-assessment framework are focused on the individual employee, whereas the last question is focused on career choices within the organization. Of course, the specific questions asked of employees during the self-assessment process can be customized to meet the needs of the organization and intended audience, and subject matter experts may be used to develop the appropriate checklist of responses.[13]

Once the employee has completed the self-assessment, the next step is to summarize and integrate the results, focusing on the key values, interests, strengths, and significant experiences. Figure 8.2 illustrates what this can look like.

Employees will want to consider several additional questions during the self-assessment process:

- What is your ideal job? This job should do the following:
  - » Leverage your strengths
  - » Align with your interests and values
  - » Leverage your experiences
- What is the path to your ideal job?
- What are your gaps to obtaining that job?
  - » Competency gaps
  - » Experience gaps

Table 8.2 Framework for Self-Directed Career Exploration

Self-Assessment Questions	
What is important to me? What do I value?	☑ Achievement ☑ Teamwork ☑ Innovation ☑ Personal Wealth ☑ Other _____
What do I enjoy in a job?	☑ Structure ☑ Autonomy ☑ Managing Others ☑ Working on a team ☑ Highly technical ☑ Other _____
What are my strengths? What are my development needs?	☑ Problem Solving ☑ Technical Skills ☑ Written Communication ☑ Motivating Other ☑ Other _____
What are my significant experiences?	☑ Managed Others ☑ Technical Skills ☑ Operations Experience ☑ Sales And Marketing Experience ☑ Other _____
What types of career development opportunities will best meet my needs?	☑ Cross-Functional Assignments/Rotations ☑ Mentoring ☑ Technical Training ☑ Leadership Development ☑ Other _____

The summary of values, interests, competencies, and experiences, combined with responses to the questions above, will help employees identify potential "ideal jobs" and establish an appropriate career development course of action.

Develop an Action Plan. Once the ideal role(s) has been identified, the next step is to build a career development plan. Similar to a traditional development plan, it focuses on strengths, development needs, development actions and goals, and timing of those actions. However, career development plans have a longer-term outlook than more narrowly focused, job-specific development plans. For the best results, employees should be counseled to align their career-focused development activities as closely as possible with their job-focused development activities. Human resources should take this opportunity to remind employees that their next role cannot be a consideration until current performance goals are met or exceeded. In addition HR

Figure 8.2

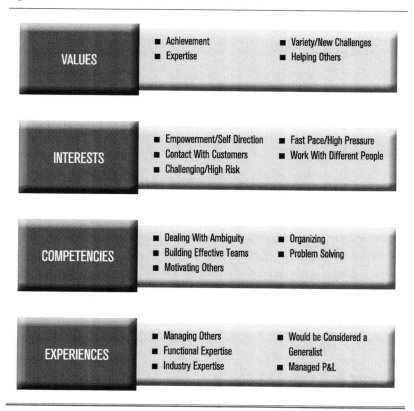

leaders should emphasize the different types of development activities that can be incorporated into the development plan:

- Expand the scope/complexity of role
- Build new skills/abilities/competencies
- Change job function (lateral move)
- Take a cross-functional assignment
- Participate in special programs (e.g., professional development programs or supplemental training)
- Obtain a promotion (but remember, it is not all about promotions!)

Traditionally, the career development process is incorporated into the overall performance management process. This practice can be effective, but leaders run the risk of having a difficult performance discussion and then trying to switch gears and squeeze in a career-development talk at the end of the meeting. Given the importance of career development, we recommend distinguishing career discussions from performance discussions to ensure that the focus is entirely on employee development needs and growth/advancement opportunities.

Execute the plan. The final step is for the employee to execute the plan. At this stage, ownership clearly falls in the lap of the employee. Managers and HR professionals will play a support role in the process, but ultimately employees are accountable for following through with their career development plan.

The process we have outlined above is not the only career development solution. However, this approach is extremely useful for organizations in which career development is viewed as a partnership between employees and the organization and employees take an active role in managing their own careers.

Case Study – Feeding America

Feeding America, a not-for-profit organization, recently revised its performance management cycle to focus on career development. Based on an evaluation of their employee survey data, the senior HR team identified a need to further define and enhance the career development process. The new development process focused on both immediate, job-specific development for employees in their current roles as well as longer-term, career-focused development. The HR team sought to deploy a development process and supporting tools that were simple, practical to use, and integrated into their existing performance management process. The career development process we developed was conducted separately from their annual performance review to keep the entire focus of the meeting on employee development. Furthermore, the process leveraged and integrated their existing content (e.g., competency models and career maps). Using the Career ADVICE approach described in the previous section, Feeding America created a customized career development process. The steps followed to create their process and the supporting tools are described in Figure 8.3.

Once the process and content were designed, Feeding America's performance management technology vendor incorporated the new process and tools into the existing software application. The final step was to launch the new tools using face-to-face and webinar training sessions for managers and employees. To make the process truly business-focused, key metrics were first developed to help demonstrate the impact of the upgraded career development process:

Figure 8.3

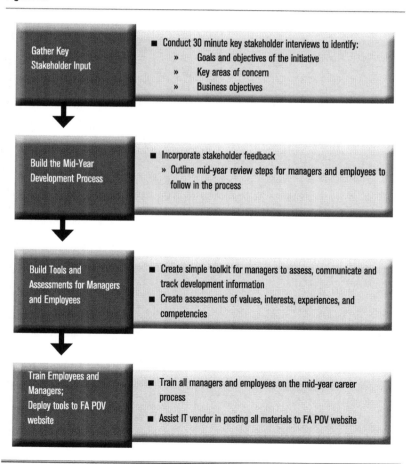

- Significant improvement in employee opinions of career and training opportunities
- Reduced overall turnover and high-performer turnover
- Improved leadership pipeline — specifically having multiple ready-now candidates for all key positions in the organization or specific plans and career paths in place for ready-now candidates

The career development process resulted in well-above benchmark performance on employee opinions of career development opportunities as well as historically low turnover for the organization, particularly among high performers. Finally, the career development program strengthened the organization's leadership pipeline, helping to ensure that ready-now candidates were in place with strong career plans to continue their development for future roles.

Practical Tips

We have summarized a list of practical tips to share with employees as they take ownership of their careers and execute their career development plan:

- Performance drives everything — you must perform in your current role before you even think about the next role.
- Work on shoring up competency or experience gaps.
- Develop an expertise.
- Be proactive — do not wait on your manager or the organization.
- Be patient and build skills that increase your marketability.
- Network with successful people.
- Treat your boss as your most deserving client.
- Do everything asked of you. . . then ask for more.
- Be consistent in your relationships and in how you treat people.
- Ensure you ask for feedback and then act on it.
- Performance management conversations are keys to your success.
- Constantly expand your sphere of influence.
- Build your technical expertise and your leadership skills.
- Know the industry.
- Do not worry about just "moving up" — sideways works wonders too.
- Lead from the front and be seen as one that energizes others.
- Build new relationships and strengthen existing ones.
- Embrace change and take risks.
- Strive for excellence and avoid mediocrity.

HR leaders play a substantial role in the career process as well. Some key activities and tips include the following:

- Work directly with key stakeholders to create and rollout a well-defined career process.

- Train front-line and senior leaders on their roles and responsibilities in the process.

- Train front-line and senior leaders on how to conduct effective career development discussions.

- Train employees on how to use any tools that are created (for example, to assess values, interests, and experience) and educate them on their role in the career development process.

- Create strong objective and subjective metrics to measure performance. Connect all metrics to business outcomes (e.g. productivity and turnover).

- Report to senior leaders the success of the program by highlighting the direct linkage between metrics and business outcomes.

CHAPTER 9

Leadership Development

Interest in and spending on leadership development has grown exponentially over the last two decades. The increased focus on leadership development has resulted from organizations looking for better ways to deal with competitive pressures, responding quickly and flexibly to rapidly changing conditions, and using new technologies to their benefit.[1] As corporate spending on leadership development increases, HR leaders are facing greater pressure to demonstrate a return on investment for their leadership development initiatives.[2] Executives know intuitively that leadership development is valuable; however, HR leaders are the ones to execute effectively and demonstrate that value.

In this chapter, we present what researchers have discovered that can help HR professionals develop better leaders and more effective leadership development programs. Additionally, we discuss best practices and key tenets from our history of developing leaders and provide insights on how to create a business-focused leadership development program. Finally, we spend time focusing on executive assessment and coaching and the ways in which such practices can be integrated with and used to enhance leadership development initiatives.

What the Research Tells Us

Leadership development has been defined as "broadening the capacity of an individual to be effective in leadership roles and processes."[3] More specifically, it involves helping to develop the knowledge, skills, and abilities that organizations value with regard to leadership. Researchers have tried to make a distinction in the terms used to talk about leadership development. They have suggested that distinguishing between *leader* development and *leadership* development is crucial. Leader development focuses on individual leaders and increasing their specific capacity to lead. This process involves the acquisition of skills, self-awareness, and motivation to lead others. Examples of leader development initiatives include coaching programs, 360-developmental feedback, and assessment centers. Leadership development, on the other hand, focuses on the organization's collective leadership capacity and involves building relationships and team capabilities across the organization.[4] Examples of leadership development initiatives include talent management processes, pipeline or succession planning systems, and training exercises focused on teambuilding. The distinction between *leader* and *leadership* development brings to light the need to focus on both the individual and organizational level to maximize the impact of development initiatives.

In addition, it is necessary to carefully consider the tools and training tactics used as part of any leadership development program. In most organizations, exclusively classroom-based leadership development programs are rapidly becoming a thing of the past. Companies have begun implementing a wide array of leadership training practices to maximize learning outcomes. Such comprehensive leadership development initiatives go beyond the classroom to encompass the leader's work environment and interactions with employees and peers. Though formal training may be a necessary element of leadership development, developmental experiences have been found to have the greatest impact when they are linked to or embedded in a leader's daily work activities.[5] Experiences such as forming developmental relationships (e.g., executive coaching), action learning, and 360-degree feedback are increasingly becoming key aspects of leader development. These experiences should build upon one another such that learning from early experiences serves as the foundation for navigating later, more challenging, experiences. Furthermore, like every other process we have explored so far, these developmental experiences must be tailored to meet the unique needs of the leader. For example, a non-leader employee who is being developed into a leader would focus on key areas of basic "blocking and tackling" (e.g. time management, delegation, giving feedback, and motivation) so that he or she can make the move from individual contributor to leader. In contrast, a long-time middle manager could focus more on strategic thinking and developing or coaching others.

Building Business-Focused Leadership Development Programs

In building the business case for leadership development in your organization, first develop an understanding of the issues and challenges that your executives have identified as significant to the business. The Society for Human Resource Management (SHRM) recently interviewed hundreds of global human resources and non-HR leaders regarding leadership-specific challenges facing their organizations and found some interesting results:

- While 58 percent of respondents expect their organizations to grow over the next 10 years, all expect hiring, retaining, and developing leaders to become more difficult.

- Only 40 percent of respondents reported that their organizations had a formalized succession or executive coaching program in place.
- Only 54 percent reported having a process in place to identify potential leaders.[6]

HR leaders are well positioned to create leadership development programs that tackle the issues identified by the leaders in the SHRM study. Specific initiatives that HR leaders may consider include adding and growing leaders to meet business growth expectations, putting in place formalized succession planning processes, examining the value of executive coaching in their organization, and creating a comprehensive program to identify future leaders within the employee population.

In addition to the challenges identified by the executives in the SHRM study, also keep in mind the specific challenges that HR leaders face when implementing leadership development programs:

- A rapidly changing, competitive environment
- Knowledge retention
- Pressure to innovate
- Potential generational differences
- Pressure to cut costs
- Lack of understanding of experiences needed for future roles
- Evaluating leadership development effectiveness

In the rest of this chapter, we will provide insight on how to address the challenges expressed by both executives and HR leaders and to ensure the successful design and implementation of leadership development initiatives in your organization.

Effective Execution

The four key steps to designing and implementing a business-focused leadership development program are outlined below.

Build the Leadership Strategy

When creating a leadership development program, first explicitly outline the organization's leadership strategy, which must be derived from the overarching business strategy. The leadership strategy will provide the "blueprint" for the actual program. Numerous factors will influence your leadership strategy:

- External business trends
- Key business strategies
- Required organizational capabilities and competencies
- Leadership and business priorities

- The organization's culture
- Performance objectives

Here are some additional questions to ask as you formulate your leadership strategy: How will the business strategy impact the organizational design in the next 3-5 years? Given the business strategy over the next 3-5 years, what types of leaders are needed (for example, what are the experiences required or competencies needed)? How will future leadership roles be filled (e.g., internal hires, external hires, or a mix)?

Identify the Goals of the Program

Once a clear leadership development strategy is in place, the goals of the program need to be clearly articulated. A key step in the process, these goals will provide the foundation for design and evaluation of the program's effectiveness. As an example, your program goals may focus on the following:

- Improving decision-making for promotions or leadership assignments
- Streamlining talent identification and planning processes
- Enhancing succession planning initiatives
- Providing input for significant reorganizations
- Developing high potentials or critical leaders
- Improving leadership team alignment and group dynamics

Build the Program

The next step in the process is to identify the program components that will most effectively accomplish the previously established goals. A variety of components can be included, but they must be selected carefully and with purpose to achieve the desired goals. Some of the possible components that could be used include the following:

- Assessment, feedback, and development planning (e.g., 360-degree feedback)
- Coaching
- Action learning teams focused on real business issues
- Job assignments or rotations
- Group learning activities
- Team building and development
- Exposure to the strategic business agenda

We discuss several of these components in greater detail in the next section. By incorporating the appropriate number of leadership development components, you will create a more comprehensive, sustainable program.

This step also involves identifying the program participants. The leadership strategy will help guide the selection of appropriate participants. For some organizations, the focus may be on executive-level leaders, whereas others may wish to focus on leaders in critical roles across levels of the organization. In addition to considering leaders' operating level or position, also weigh the developmental readiness of those chosen to participate. Are participants motivated to improve and receptive to constructive feedback? Do participants have the capacity to develop into a better leader? The answers to these and similar questions will help guide who is chosen to participate in the program and which program components should be included to maximize learning and development outcomes.

Implement and Evaluate the Program

Significant time is spent building the leadership development program and establishing goals — equally critical is to determine whether the goals have been met. Create a comprehensive, but not overwhelming, scorecard to see if the goals were met and to showcase the impact that the program is having on the organization. Some sample metrics are provided in Table 9.1, but remember that the metrics you use should be based on the specific goals you established for your leadership development program.

Donald L. Kirkpatrick's model of program evaluation provides a strong framework from which to evaluate the effectiveness of your leadership development program.[7] This model includes four levels of evaluation: reaction, learning, transfer, and results. Reactions gauge the participants' perceptions of the program's success. This type of measurement is important because, at a minimum, you want the participants to like the program and to believe that it is having a positive impact. The learning level includes measures of the new knowledge acquired and retained. Learning can be examined at intervals or at the conclusion of the program. The transfer level looks at the application of the program's content in the working environment and can be measured via follow-up 360-degree assessments, change in employee opinion scores, and/or follow-up interviews with peers, subordinates, or superiors. The results level is evaluated in terms of the impact on the bottom line (such as increased revenue, better

Table 9.1 Sample Leadership Development Program Scorecard Metrics

Milestone completion
Retention of participants
Performance of participants
Change in behavior
Ready-now replacements for critical roles
Compare the performance of leaders in the program to those not in the program

performance, higher quality, or better customer service). The process can be carried out by examining direct changes in bottom-line results via before-and-after analysis of program participants and/or by comparing bottom-line results (for example, sales dollars or customer satisfaction ratings) of those who participated in the training to those of nonparticipants.

Components of the Leadership Development Program

Leadership development should not happen in a vacuum — it should be directly connected to both career development and succession planning (see Figure 9.1). You may choose among several components to utilize in your leadership development program, including assessment, executive coaching, action learning, group learning activities, and job assignments and rotations. The most effective leadership development programs include many or all of these components. We discuss these components in greater detail below.

Figure 9.1

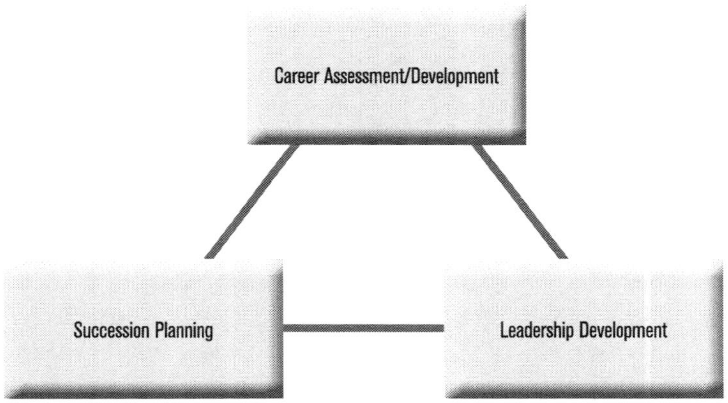

Assessment. An assessment of participants' skills and abilities comes first and should be comprehensive so that all the learning and coaching can be as customized as possible. Our integrated approach to assessment is shown in Figure 9.2.

An integrated suite of assessments provides a comprehensive picture of the participants' skills, traits, experiences, and potential to move into future roles. Each assessment represents a different aspect of leaders that impacts their behaviors and ultimately their success. The various types of assessments include the following:

- Behavior-based assessment, which includes a quantitative 360-degree assessment (see Chapter 5 for more details) and a behavior-based interview of key stakeholders
- A biographical interview of the leader, which includes questions related to significant experiences, achievements, and career aspirations
- Personality assessment (e.g., Hogan Personality Inventory, 16PF)
- Cognitive ability test (e.g., Watson-Glaser)
- Review of experiences, which includes identifying the experiences a leader has and the ones he or she does not have, as well as the key experiences required for future target roles. A sample Experience Framework is shown in Table 9.2 and can be used in your front-end assessment to discover the experience levels of your program's participants. The Experience Framework should be customized to reflect the various functions and roles within your organization. The framework can be completed by the leader during a career development assessment or as part of the suite of assessments recommended above before beginning a leadership development program. The results will provide leaders and HR representatives with the opportunity to uncover gaps in leaders' experiences and to create customized development plans to fill those gaps to help leaders prepare for future roles.

Figure 9.2

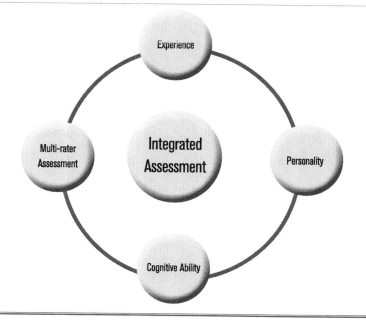

Table 9.2

Developed a functional expertise	Obtained industry expertise
Performed multiple roles within your function	Risk Management experience
Would be considered a generalist within function	Sales and Marketing experience
Would be considered a specialist within function	Led cross-function project/team
Managed others	Led significant organizational change
Managed managers	Operations experience
Managed large projects	Managed products/service lines
P&L experience	Led significant innovation

Once all the assessments are collected, organizations should enlist an objective outsider (external or internal) to integrate all the material and create a report that presents (1) the actual data from each assessment component, (2) an executive summary of the results, and (3) recommendations on how to take action based on the results. This report is typically presented to leaders by their designated coach at the beginning of the leadership program.

Executive coaching. Executive coaching has been defined as

a helping relationship formed between a client who has managerial authority and responsibility in an organization and a consultant (external or internal) who uses a wide variety of behavioral techniques and methods to help the client achieve a mutually identified set of goals to improve his or her professional performance and personal satisfaction and, consequently, to improve the effectiveness of the client's organization within a formally defined coaching agreement.[8]

This process is typically called *executive* coaching because, due to cost and time constraints, it is oftentimes a program reserved for executives. However, coaching of any leader in an organization can and should follow the same process outlined here.

The key elements of executive coaching relationships are listed below:

- One-on-one counseling on issues related to work or professional development
- Valid assessments of the client's strengths and opportunities for improvement
- Purposeful goal-setting and follow-up as a means of producing desired behavioral changes and improving managerial effectiveness

Executive coaches must have a clear understanding of their client's issue or development needs as well as knowledge of the organizational context and culture and be able to translate this understanding and knowledge into an actionable and relevant development plan for their client. Clients, in turn, must be open to honest feedback, accept the need for change, and be accountable for following through on their development plan. Understanding the context and needs of the coachee is relevant regardless of whether the organization uses external or internal coaches.

A variety of approaches to executive coaching exist, and within each approach are a number of tools and techniques that coaches may employ with their clients.

Approaches to executive coaching. The following are the most frequently employed approaches to executive coaching:

- *Psychodynamic approach.* This approach is intended to help executives better understand their unconscious thoughts, feelings, and internal psychological states.

- *Behaviorist approach.* The focus is on the client's observable behaviors rather than on internal psychological states.

- *Person-centered approach.* The focus is on clients taking personal responsibility for their behaviors and the associated consequences rather than on attributing any issues to external causes.

- *Cognitive therapy approach.* This approach centers on recognizing and changing patterns of thought. Coaches work with their clients to uncover and change dysfunctional or counterproductive thought processes.

- *Systems-oriented approach.* This holistic approach involves a focus on the individual, group, and organizational influences on the client's behavior. Coaches become knowledgeable about the organizational system, including the mission, culture, and organizational networks before identifying their client's development needs and building action plans.[9]

HR leaders should evaluate which approach will work best in their organization and which will be most useful for specific executives. When assessing potential vendors, inquire about the approach they utilize. Selecting a vendor that uses an approach that would not be seen as credible in your organization could undermine the value of the coaching engagement.

Outcomes of Executive Coaching

Irrespective of the particular coaching approach, the primary goal of executive coaching is to produce changes in managerial behavior that improve individual and organizational performance. Although consultants often tout the benefits of coaching interventions, rigorous empirical assessments of coaching outcomes are few and far between. Research has shown that fewer than 10 percent of organizations assess the impact of coaching on performance. In one survey of executive coaches, the majority indicated that they obtained subjective feedback from clients but did not assess the linkage between coaching and individual or organizational performance.[10]

The few empirical studies of executive coaching that do exist generally suggest that coaching helps executives gain self-knowledge and self-confidence, learn new skills, build meaningful leadership abilities (for example, change management/adaptability and teambuilding/relationship building), and improve self-rated performance. In a study of executives participating in a coaching and 360-degree feedback process, researchers found that the combination of one-on-one coaching and multi-rater feedback increased leadership effectiveness by up to 60 percent.[11] Other research found that managers who worked with an executive coach were more likely than those who had not worked with a coach to establish specific goals, solicit feedback, and receive improved performance ratings one year after the coaching relationship concluded.[12]

Together, these results suggest that executive coaching has a positive impact on individual attitudes and performance. However, research has not demonstrated the effect of executive coaching on objective organizational performance. Merely "liking" your coach is not evidence of impact; the investments made in coaching must drive bottom-line organizational results.

Group Learning

Periodic group learning sessions focus on issues that are directly related to the business and provide opportunities for participants to connect the program to the overarching leadership and organizational strategies. Showing a senior team the connection between the data you collected on the assessments and the topics covered in the group learning sessions is critical to obtaining and sustaining buy-in. The education you provide in the group learning sessions should focus on important topics such as creating a strong development path for the senior team as a group, defining leadership for the organization, or changing group behaviors. The topics covered in the group learning session should leverage participants' strengths while addressing their development needs. Ultimately, the group learning sessions can create a group dynamic that encourages partnership and shared achievement.

Action Learning Teams

Researchers have defined action learning teams as a set of organized development practices in which crucial real-time organizational problems are tackled.[13] In practice, action learning teams are highly interactive learning exercises during which leadership teams are assigned real strategic business problems. Action learning teams work together to find solutions, present findings and recommendations, and field tough questions on their proposals. Coaches and other senior leaders have the opportunity to observe leaders in a group setting where they can provide rich feedback on how they presented the material and fielded questions as well as on the thoroughness of their research and proposed solutions. The action learning teams also provide a chance to build stronger relationships among peers. Some key things to remember when incorporating action learning teams are listed below:

- Team assignments must be thoughtful. Assign individuals to teams who would not normally interact with one another in the regular course of business and who have diverse knowledge and skill sets.

- Personality derailers will emerge. These include counterproductive interpersonal behaviors such as excessively controlling situations, passively-aggressively addressing conflict, or dominating social interactions. Observations by managers or coaches help ensure that when derailers emerge, they can be managed and mitigated.

- Structure the process with deadlines and presentations. The action learning teams should not go on without an ending. Guidelines, deadlines, and a final presentation can be scheduled for the "next" quarterly group learning session.

Job Assignments or Rotations

Longer-term leadership development programs often include a job assignment or rotational component. Such components offer the best chance for participants to gain new knowledge, build stronger cross-functional networks, and develop novel approaches to strategic problem-solving. The goals of job assignments are generally to do the following:

- Turn specialists into generalists.
- Build cross-functional managerial skills and abilities.
- Acquire key skills required for a future target role (for example, gaining experience in finance before proceeding to an executive-level leadership position).

Keep in mind two important aspects of job assignments:

- Be careful not to take a leader out of a role until he or she has the opportunity to succeed or fail — just getting a taste of the new role is not enough to maximize the learning experience.

- This process must be structured and planned such that participants know what to expect during and after their rotational assignment. Linking job assignments or rotations to your succession planning process will help to maximize their effectiveness.

Case Study: Randstad US

Randstad US is a wholly owned subsidiary of Randstad Holding nv, a $17.7 billion global provider of HR services and the second largest staffing organization in the world. Randstad US has over 3,100 employees. We worked with the company to design and implement a comprehensive approach to developing its entire senior leadership team. This process meant not only focusing on individual leader performance but also addressing the overall functioning of the senior leadership team and the knowledge, skills, and abilities they needed to more effectively run the organization. The president of the organization was a participant, thus helping to ensure the success of the leadership development program from the outset. She was bought in from the start and was actively involved as a participant — not as an observer. Figure 9.3 represents the process that was undertaken to build leaders at Randstad.

Figure 9.3

Program Design		Assessment & Feedback		Group Learning Sessions		Action Learning Teams

The Randstad program began with a thorough review of the business strategy, the business needs, the leadership competency model, and the most recent employee opinion survey results to help shape the design and direction of the program. Based on our review of these key pieces of information, we designed and launched the assessment and feedback phase.

Assessment and Feedback

Figure 9.4 shows the specific components of the assessment and feedback portion of the program and how these were utilized as the foundation of the leadership development process.

For Randstad, we built a customized online 360-degree assessment based on its leadership competency model. In addition, we created customized 360-degree stakeholder interviews that were also focused on the competency model but that allowed us to get richer, more specific feedback from peers, employees, customers, the boss and other partners. The biographical interviews were 2-hour, in-depth interviews between the coaches and the participants during which coaches learned more about the participants' experiences, achievements, self-awareness, strengths, weaknesses, and development opportunities. The interviews were also a chance for the coaches and participants to begin to build rapport with each other. We also conducted an online personality assessment to understand participants' personality traits and possible derailers.

Our Integrated Leadership Assessment Report™ provides a comprehensive way of integrating all the assessment results and sharing them with each participant. The report provides an executive summary of the results with a focus on strengths and development opportunities. It then goes into more detail and reviews the data collected from each of the assessments in the process. The report was shared with the participant only — no one else had access to the report. The participants were able to share the report if they so desired but were not required to do so as part of the program.

Figure 9.4

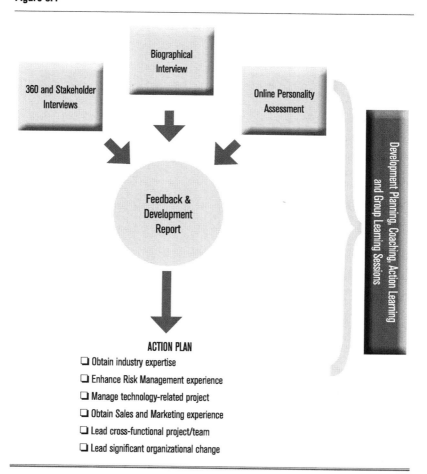

Program Design

We implemented group learning sessions focused on key senior leadership development areas. These focus areas were purely data-driven, as they came directly from the cumulative data collected on the personality assessments, the online 360-degree assessment, the stakeholder interviews, and the business strategy. The group learning sessions lasted from 4-6 hours during each quarterly senior team meeting. During the first group learning session, the group's cumulative 360-degree assessment and personality data were presented to dig deeper into the group dynamics and to examine how to overcome their obstacles.

The coaching that was provided focused on creating a specific development plan derived from the integrated assessment report. All participants, with their coaches, created a development plan after debriefing their report. A one-hour coaching meeting was held once a month between the coach and the participant, with intermittent coaching phone calls on an as-needed basis. Coaches attempted to be readily available via phone should participants encounter challenging situations or find themselves in need of advice.

Action learning teams were focused on strategic business issues currently facing the organization. In addition to asking participants to generate realistic solutions to six distinct business issues, we set the following specific goals for their action learning process:

- Facilitate strategic decision-making for the organization.
- Get everyone's ideas on the table.
- Make an informed decision as a group.
- Influence others in the organization.
- Learn from peer perspectives.
- Build new pockets of teamwork.

We also set the following clear guidelines for the presentations conducted by each team during the quarterly group learning meetings:

- Clearly defined methodology for gathering facts and information
- Clearly stated objectives
- A decision with a compelling business case
- Full strategy and tactical plan
- A clear, concise story with a defined model and a focused, short presentation

The coaches were present during all action learning team meetings to observe and assess the teams' interactions and their presentations and were able to offer developmental feedback to all participants. The senior team's discussion of the solutions proposed by each action learning team resulted in the implementation of all six proposals. The specific goals for the action learning teams were met, and now a great opportunity exists to cascade this type of activity to lower levels of leadership across the organization.

Impact Criteria

The impact of the program was assessed and measured on multiple levels:

- Leader "Employee Opinion Survey" Score Improvement (i.e., improvement in key areas on which coaches and participants focused)
- Improved Retention of High Performers and High Potentials
- Executive Team Member Individual Improvement (as measured by a follow-up 360 assessment)
- Improvement in the Talent Pipeline (i.e., percent with plan to develop ready-now replacement and percent with ready-now replacements)

Ultimately, the leadership development program was not only "liked" by participants, but it also improved the level of teamwork among senior team members and resulted in more informed strategic decision-making. In addition, this program helped Randstad retain high-performing employees and fill their ready-now talent pipeline.

By taking a comprehensive approach to leadership that began with examining the needs of the business and the business strategy and included thorough up-front assessments, group and individual coaching, and key metrics linked to business outcomes, the organization was able to achieve the specific results that it set out to accomplish.

Leadership development programs can provide a valuable resource to organizations for managing their human capital and ensuring that organizational capabilities are aligned with the business strategy. These types of programs are most successful when the organization takes a systematic approach to their design and execution. Over the years, the sophistication and effectiveness of these programs has evolved significantly. By leveraging "lessons learned," best practices, and applied organizational research, organizations can build effective leadership development programs to help achieve their business goals.

Practical Tips

Designing and implementing development initiatives that effectively address individual as well as organizational leadership needs can be intimidating. The following practical tips help to ensure that leader and leadership development initiatives are well integrated with existing programs or processes, supported by key stakeholders, and appropriately structured so as to maximize their impact:

- *Align with business strategy.* The best leadership development systems are driven by business strategy. The first step in any development process is to identify the business strategy and the goals of the program. Then, and only then, can leader/ leadership development planning begin.
- *Engage executive-level stakeholders.* Endorsement from high-level leaders lends credibility to leadership development efforts and helps increase buy-in from lower-level employees.
- *Ensure leader readiness.* Successful leadership development efforts are dependent upon the leader's developmental readiness, desire to learn, and the capacity to develop into a better leader. In selecting leaders to participate in a leadership development initiative, careful consideration must be given to their readiness and willingness to learn.
- *Focus on tailored leadership competencies.* Leader/leadership development initiatives should be designed around a core set of leadership competencies that are aligned with the specific goals and strategy of the organization. The same broad set of competencies should apply to leaders within the organization; however, the specific skills and abilities within each competency may need to be tailored to reflect variations in leaders' responsibilities and span of control across different organizational levels.
- *Invest in systems, not just individuals.* To be most effective, leader and leadership development efforts need to target all levels of leadership, not just executives. Furthermore, development initiatives should address leadership needs at both the individual and organizational level.
- *Apply a comprehensive and ongoing approach.* Leader/leadership development is most valuable when accomplished in the reality of leaders' work context. Embedding developmental components in leaders' day-to-day work enhances the job relevance of developmental experiences and increases the transfer of learning to the job.
- *Integrate with other programs/initiatives.* The development of new leadership competencies (for example, through action learning, coaching, or training) helps prepare leaders for more complex future roles within the organization. As a result, leader and leadership development are often linked to succession planning, which we discuss in detail in Chapter 10. However, the most effective leadership development programs are also integrated with a wide variety of other programs or initiatives, including management training, executive development, performance management, and the cultivation and management of high-potential talent.

- *Focus on results.* Empirical evidence suggests that complex leadership skills can indeed be learned, and such learning has been found to have a positive impact on individuals and organizations. To demonstrate the value of leader/leadership development and ensure ongoing support for key stakeholders, the impact of your initiative must be assessed. This involves linking the initiative to both the learning and performance of individual leaders and bottom-line organizational outcomes (e.g., reduced turnover or ROI).

CHAPTER 10

Succession Planning

Succession planning has evolved over the years from an approach focused almost exclusively on having a replacement ready for the CEO to a comprehensive plan for assessing and managing talent moves across multiple levels — focusing on management positions and critical jobs. Succession planning has many definitions, running the gamut from "an on-going, equitable plan to develop and prepare employees for leadership positions at all levels throughout the organization" to "the process of identifying high potential employees, evaluating and honing their skills and abilities, and preparing them for advancement into positions which are key to the success of business operations and objectives."[1] In some cases, the focus remains on high-potential employees; in other cases, the focus is more broadly on talent across all levels of the organization. Either way, succession planning must become more comprehensive and be linked directly to business outcomes and business strategy, with a goal of creating a strong pipeline of leaders across the organization.

What the Research Tells Us

The research demonstrates that companies with effective succession planning practices and policies have higher returns on sales, investments, assets, and equity.[2] Succession planning has been identified as having an indirect impact on productivity and gross returns on assets.[3] Although studies have provided evidence for the relationship between succession planning and desired business outcomes, few have addressed critical components of effective succession planning processes. In one of the few applied studies to date, researchers examined a variety of industries around the world and found that firms with "best-in-class" succession planning processes shared the following characteristics:

- A formalized process for identifying high-performance workers
- Regular reviews of performance and progress of high potentials
- Clear linkages between leadership development, succession planning, and business objectives
- Clearly defined success profiles for key positions[4]

In the following sections, we discuss how to design and implement effective succession planning processes that include the "best-in-class" characteristics and help drive bottom-line organizational results.

Effective Design and Execution

Although the scope of succession planning initiatives differs from organization to organization, the basic process for designing and implementing an effective succession planning process is largely the same. As noted in the limited applied research, the key steps to designing and implementing an effective succession plan are as follows:

- *Establish present and future leadership roles and objectives.* This step deals primarily with aligning succession planning with the organization's long-term strategy and mission. The questions that need to be addressed here include the following:
  - » What will the business look like in the next 1-5 years?
  - » Which business goals and operations will be the most important?
  - » Will any job functions be consolidated?
  - » Will workload change?
  - » Are any new positions needed?
- *Identify high-potential employees.* Identification of high potentials depends on the set of organizational needs identified in the first step. Avoid "like the current incumbent" approaches, as future needs will almost always be different from solutions currently in place. Instead, organizations should apply a consistent and objective assessment process to identify high-potential employees. The best approaches to the identification of high potentials are structured around the competencies included in the organization's definition of leadership.
- *Evaluate the strengths and weaknesses of high-potential employees.* The next step is to evaluate both the strengths and development needs of high-potential employees. This evaluation can be accomplished through 360-degree performance feedback, behavioral assessments, or evaluations conducted by external consultants.
- *Build and review individual development plans.* High-potential employees should work with their manager and other key stakeholders to build a development plan tailored to their needs. This plan can include, for example, internal mentoring, technical and nontechnical training, and executive coaching. These plans should be reviewed on a regular basis and adjusted as needed.
- *Identify positions without internal successors.* These positions should be filled externally. We will elaborate on the choice between internal and external hiring in the next section.
- *Assess the succession planning process.* Assessing the relationship between the succession planning initiative and critical business objectives (for example,

high-potential retention and ready-now replacements) is imperative. Doing so helps quantify the value of the succession planning process and to demonstrate a return on investment.[5]

Internal and External Hiring in Succession Management

Most companies use a mix of both internal and external hiring. The goal is to train and develop employees from within to move into high-level positions while simultaneously keeping track of current or future jobs for which the demand exceeds available internal talent. These positions will need to be filled from outside the organization.

Internal succession planning often helps limit the higher costs (for example, hiring-of-an-executive-headhunter costs and additional marketing and recruitment costs) and steeper internal learning curves associated with hiring external talent. It can reduce the risk of employing an individual from outside the organization who may not have broad industry experience, lacks company knowledge, or may be incompatible with the company's culture. Of course, internal candidates are not without their own risks. Limiting potential hires to the internal candidate pool, by definition, means fewer options. Employees who have worked within the organization for a number of years may lack fresh ideas or be unable to take a different perspective on challenging issues. Furthermore, if dramatic organizational overhaul is required, then being an insider can be a drawback.[6] Research suggests that outsiders may perform better when brought in to help poor-performing organizations.[7] One reason might be that these leaders ageless apprehensive about making major changes that meet with organizational resistance.

Common Obstacles to Successful Succession Planning

Organizations often encounter several obstacles when attempting to design and execute a succession planning process. In one study, organizations cited the following as the most common obstacles: other business activities were seen as more important by business leaders (64 percent), senior management did not feel a sense of urgency (63 percent), and business leaders lacked management skills to execute the strategy (28 percent).[8]

Other research gives a more detailed picture of why succession planning programs may underperform. For instance, in a study of multinational companies across a range of industries with geographic regions covering North America, Africa, Asia, and Europe, the reasons for underperformance tended to focus on the people executing the process rather than on the process itself.[9] The specific obstacles cited by senior leaders included the following:

- Senior managers not spending enough high-quality time on talent management (54 percent)
- Line managers not sufficiently committed to the development of people (52 percent)
- The organization being "siloed" and not encouraging constructive cross-functional collaboration; limitations in the sharing of resources (51 percent)
- Line managers unwilling to differentiate their people as top, average, or underperformers (50 percent)
- Senior leaders in the organization not aligning the talent management strategy with the business strategy (47 percent)
- Line managers not addressing chronic underperformance effectively (45 percent)
- Succession planning and/or resource allocation processes not being rigorous enough to match the right people to the right roles (39 percent)
- The senior team not having a shared view on the most critical roles (38 percent)

The majority of the obstacles discussed above fall into four broad categories:
- Differentiating talent
- Aligning the talent strategy with the business strategy
- Implementing a rigorous planning and allocation process
- Ensuring that line managers across the organization are committed to people development

These obstacles are not insurmountable, and an HR leader with a strong process can overcome them. As we discuss in the next section, making the succession planning process business-focused helps organizations overcome each of these obstacles.

Building a Business-Focused Succession Plan

To reiterate, succession planning should be focused on talent across the organization and not solely on identifying a successor for the CEO. Planning and building a strong, sustainable pipeline of leaders for the organization is a key goal of this process.

As depicted in Figure 10.1, succession planning cannot be executed in a vacuum — career assessments and development serve as key "inputs" into the process, while custom leadership development programs for individuals, and specifically for your high-potential talent pool, help to ensure a continually developing pipeline of leaders.

Figure 10.1

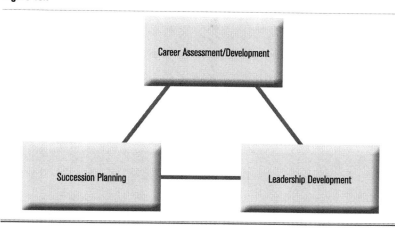

Succession planning can often fall into the trap of being a popularity contest with limited focus on the objectivity and rigor of the process and relatively weak linkages to the overall business strategy. Having talent review meetings has benefits; however, they are not sufficient in creating a business-focused succession plan. Below are the key tasks/components associated with business-focused succession plans:

- Customizing the approach to your organization (based on current and future business challenges, which can come with assumptions)
- Facilitating talent planning sessions with leaders
- Getting candidates on the "right" career path
- Linking employee data to business outcomes
- Assessing the overall health of your talent pool
- Creating leadership programs based on true talent-pool development needs as well as on individual development needs that are driving business outcomes

Our business-focused approach to succession planning helps ensure that the process is customized to the unique needs of the organization and that it is linked to critical business outcomes. We outline below the four-step approach we use with clients and include several practical tools that will help organizations be successful during each step of the process.

Assess business impact of current people data. After organizational leaders have reviewed the business strategy and identified key business metrics or outcomes that the organization hopes to achieve through the succession planning process (for example, reduction of high-performer turnover or having ready-now replacements for critical roles), the next step is to link people assessments (such as competency ratings, performance ratings, and attitude surveys) to the business metrics. This step allows organizations to identify the people factors (for example, competencies, performance levels, and attitudes) that drive the critical business outcomes. Identifying these factors involves first conducting or compiling data from assessments that capture the key competencies (for example, multi-rater/360), areas of personality (for example, valid personality assessment), employee attitudes (for example, employee opinion survey), and objective performance metrics (for example, strong performance review/performance management system). Organizations may also wish to include in this assessment phase ratings of employees' potential for advancement (for example, ready-now or ready within six months to one year). Other assessments could be conducted (e.g. cognitive ability), but for now this is a strong list with which to start.

Table 10.1 Business-focused Talent/Succession Scorecard™

Talent/Succession Scorecard	Current Performance/ Potential[a]	Critical Competencies[b]	Performance in Experiences[c]	Cog. Ability[d]	
Employee	Business Outcomes (% Effective)	Communication	Leadership	Execution	
Joe King	67%	67%	71%	75%	
Jane Smith	67%	93%	100%	53%	
Beverly Jones	69%	80%	84%	69%	
Anne Johnson	71%	91%	90%	83%	
Steve Simmons	75%	100%	100%	83%	
Bill Norder	77%	93%	88%	86%	
Paul Monroe	80%	97%	90%	87%	
Jill Stevenson	83%	94%	93%	93%	
Ben Stevens	83%	95%	94%	86%	
Average Element Score[h]	83%	92%	94%	85%	
Overall Talent Pool Health[i]	81%				

a. Current Performance This metric is a summation of current effectiveness-to-goal on business outcomes as demonstrated on the current performance review.

b. Critical Competencies This metric displays the competencies that have been shown to have the greatest cost-effect impact on overall business performance.

c. Critical Experiences This metric shows the overall business performance achieved in each of the critical experiences on the career path.

d. Cognitive Ability This score is the percentile achieved by the individual on a validated cognitive ability assessment.

e. Employee Survey This metric shows the previous 5-year average that the leader achieved on the employee opinion survey.

The next step is to conduct the cause-effect analysis to identify the factors that drive business outcomes. Align the data for each individual leader to connect his or her competencies, personality, or other characteristics to the key business outcomes for which each leader is held accountable. This analytic rigor prioritizes the organization's goals and adds a level of depth beyond having only the opinions (and biases) of key stakeholders in the succession planning process. Furthermore, this data-driven process helps organizational leaders overcome the challenges associated with differentiating talent and ensures that the key factors driving business outcomes are at the forefront of talent decisions.

Build and customize the Talent/Succession Scorecard™. The next step is to build and customize the Talent/Succession Scorecard™. We provide an example of the Talent/Succession Scorecard™ in Table 10.1.

Employee Survey[a]	Potential[f]	Individual Talent Health[g]			
Critical Exp. #1 (Dir.)	Assessment Score	5 Year Average			
29%	58%	63%	29%	25%	565
80%	0%	75%	33%	25%	63%
64%	69%	50%	48%	25%	66%
81%	91%	84%	58%	33%	79%
58%	100%	88%	92%	50%	84%
82%	87%	77%	23%	33%	76%
93%	93%	75%	27%	75%	83%
79%	0%	89%	76%	75%	79%
100%	95%	82%	79%	67%	88%
78%	78%	76%	58%	63%	81%

f. Potential This metric is the current assessment of the individual's potential by senior leadership.

g. Individual Talent Health This metric displays the overall 'health' of the individual leader. It averages their scores horizontally across all of the scorecard elements.

h. Average Element Score This metric allows senior leadership to view strengths and weaknesses across the organization in each of the critical talent areas. This score is averaged vertically on each critical area.

i. Overall Talent/Succession Pool Health This metric is a standalone measure of the overall "health" of the talent population, on a scale of 0–100 percent

This scorecard is completely focused on what drives the business because it displays only those key areas of performance and behaviors (the "what" and the "how") that were shown to have a significant impact on business outcomes (in the first step above). By clearly depicting each leader's level of performance across the categories that drive business outcomes, this approach helps calibrate ratings assigned during talent planning meetings and reduces the opportunity for biases to influence the rating process. When reading the scorecard from left to right, it quickly becomes apparent which individuals are performing well across the critical areas and which are in need of further development in their current role before they can take on new responsibilities or roles. Additionally, when reading from top to bottom within each of the key areas assessed, developmental needs that exist across the entire talent pool become obvious. The most glaring issue raised in Table 10.1 is employee attitudes, indicating that across the talent pool, employees' attitudes, which are a key driver of business outcomes, are problematic. The scorecard thus helps organizational leaders readily identify this as an area in which developmental investments are needed. Another key outcome from the scorecard is the ability to calculate an overall Talent Pool Health Score, which can be used to track progress in developing the key talent in your organization. The Talent Pool Health Score represents a summation of all talent health scores for the individuals assessed.

Finally, by incorporating information from all leaders in your organization, beyond the high potentials, the Talent/Succession Scorecard™ allows leaders to uncover individuals who are high performers on the critical business drivers who may not have been considered part of the original pool of future leaders. The highly objective nature of the scorecard also allows leaders to reconsider those originally classified as high-potential leaders, who may be vastly underperforming on competencies or results critical to the business. The scorecard will help the organization avoid missing opportunities to develop talent that may originally have been overlooked or over-investing in individuals who should not be part of the future leader talent pool.

Conduct facilitated talent planning sessions. The next step in the process is to conduct talent planning sessions. These sessions involve key decision-makers across the organization (e.g., senior leaders or managers), as well as individuals who have been identified as future talent. As we outline below, several different types of talent planning sessions and various issues should be addressed in each.

Role Clarity

Talent planning sessions afford you the opportunity to seek input on the critical roles in the organization and to reassess the activities or duties associated with each role. Specifically, subject matter experts and current incumbents (that is, employees currently holding critical roles) should be interviewed with a focus on (1) defining the top activities performed; the percent of time spent on these activities; and the activities that should be changed, added to, or removed from the role; and (2) determining if any key differences in this role across the organization exist (and why those differences exist). Gather and summarize this information prior to the talent planning session so that during the session you can facilitate a discussion that culminates in greater clarity around the knowledge, abilities, and skills required of individuals in critical roles. Such role clarity will improve alignment between succession planning efforts and the business strategy and allow you to make optimum decisions on development plans for your leaders, including those who are currently in the critical roles as well as those who may be moving into those roles in the future. Clarifying the roles will also give you the opportunity to assess the appropriateness of your career pathing strategy (if one exists) and to calibrate whether the "feeder" jobs that lead into critical roles and potential "next" jobs to follow critical roles are still appropriate.

The "9-Box" Discussion

Talent planning sessions also create opportunities to differentiate "how" employees are performing from "what" they are accomplishing on the job. This approach was made famous by GE with its "Session C" approach to leadership development, in which a 9-box exercise was utilized to rate the "what" and the "how" of employee performance.[10] The 9-box exercise has worked well and continues to work well as a way to differentiate talent. We provide a simplified example of a 9-box exercise in Table 10.2. During this exercise, employee behaviors (i.e., the "how") and results or performance (i.e., the "what") are rated by managers or senior leaders. Ratings are often assigned using a three-point scale that reflects low, average, and high levels of performance. Organizational leaders commonly use the terms (or some variation thereof) "too new to rate," "does not meet," "meets," or "exceeds" to define the various levels of performance.

Historically, 9-box rating exercises have involved a high degree of subjectivity with little data-based rigor. Using the Talent/Succession Scorecard™ as the foundation for the 9-box exercise helps organizational leaders overcome this subjectivity and focuses the rating process and succession decisions on results and behaviors that directly impact business outcomes.

Table 10.2

12-month Performance		Behaviors "The How"		
		Does Not Meet Expectations	Meets Expectations	Exceeds Expectations
Results "The What"	Exceeds Expectations	Employee 1	Employee 29 Employee 30 Employee 31 Employee 32	Employee 2 Employee 3 Employee 4
	Meets Expectations	Employee 5 Employee 6 Employee 7 Employee 8 Employee 9	Employee 10 Employee 11 Employee 12 Employee 13	Employee 14 Employee 15 Employee 16 Employee 17 Employee 18
	Does Not Meet Expectations	Employee 19 Employee 20	Employee 21 Employee 22 Employee 23 Employee 24	Employee 25 Employee 26
Too Soon to Rate	Employee 27 Employee 28			

Performance Management

The 9-box ratings and Talent/Succession Scorecard™ provide a solid foundation for performance management and help instill accountability for performance improvement, particularly for those who fell into the "does not meet expectations" category. During talent planning sessions, examine the employees who fall into the unacceptable (i.e., "does not meet") category and identify a plan of action for their development. Will they be expected to move up or out? Would particular leadership or career development opportunities (see Chapters 8 and 9) help them be more successful? It is fair to ask what the specific plan is for this group and hold the leadership accountable for executing those plans.

High-Potential Assessment

During the facilitated talent planning sessions, organizational leaders should define what high potential or "expandable" talent means and identify employees who fall into each of these categories. The former is someone who can make a one- or even two-level jump in the organization, who has the ability and capacity to take on considerable responsibility, and who would be successful in more than one critical leadership role across the organization. Individuals who can "expand" are those who can take on additional scope/scale in their role and who may also jump a level in the organization. Once high-potential and expandable talent have been identified, managers should have career conversations with these individuals (see Chapter 8) to identify appropriate developmental opportunities and discuss the high-potential/expandable employees' career goals and aspirations.

Comprehensive Talent Review

Talent planning sessions can also be used to assess the existing talent pool against the current and future needs of the organization. What are the future needs of the business? How much and what type of talent do we need to sustain success and execute on our strategy? What is the tenure of individuals in current roles? What are our current open jobs? Which individuals have said they are willing to relocate? Have we made a sufficient number of talent moves and filled necessary gaps from the last time we had a talent review? What lateral moves, promotions, or specially assigned projects have we moved our high performers and high potentials into in the last year?

Launch focused leadership development program with an emphasis on the ready-now/high-potential population. The final step is to launch a focused leadership development program that targets the high-potential and expandable talent identified in the previous steps. As we discuss more thoroughly in Chapter 9, this program may include additional executive assessments and coaching, action learning teams focused on critical business outcomes, group learning, cross-functional roles or projects, or planned job rotations. The leadership development program should help fill any organization-wide competency or skill gaps identified on the Talent/Succession Scorecard™ as well as provide individual leaders with the specific skills they need to move into future roles.

Succession Planning Metrics

As with any HR process, generic metrics that worked in one organization may not be completely appropriate for another organization. Table 10.3 provides examples of the sample metrics we have used with organizations in the past to measure the impact and success of their business-focused succession planning process.

Table 10.3 Sample Succession Planning Metrics

Percent of key positions with "Ready-Now" Candidates in the pipeline

Percent of positions that have at least two potential successors (2-deep)

Vacancies filled by internal candidates

Job performance of successors in new roles

Overall Talent Pool Health Assessment Rating and Rating Improvement

Number of expanded developmental opportunities executed for high performers (e.g. lateral moves; cross-functional projects)

Significant reduction in high performer/high potential turnover

Significant improvement in perceptions of career opportunities on the employee survey

These metrics represent a clear opportunity for HR leaders to show the value of a comprehensive succession planning process, which comes in the form of reduced turnover and higher job performance, leadership pipeline strength, and employee engagement in the career development process.

Practical Tips

- The data to link succession planning tactics to business outcomes likely already exists — take the time to engage stakeholders early in the process to make data collection easier.
- Communicate with senior leaders to understand the desired business outcomes that should be the basis for building a succession plan.
- Utilize the Scorecard approach to make the complicated analyses practical and action-oriented.
- Introduce the Scorecard approach and analyses early in the process to streamline the talent review meetings and help ensure their effectiveness.
- Highlight the need to track overall Talent Health on the Scorecard as a means of showing progress and improvement in building leaders.
- Remember to integrate a comprehensive approach to career development and leadership development with your succession planning efforts to build and sustain your talent pipeline.

CHAPTER 11

Work/Life Balance

Work/life balance has become a catch-all term to describe employees' abilities (and an organization's policies) to manage the multiple demands of their work (job roles, resources, development) and non-work interests and responsibilities(e.g., family, pets, hobbies, relationships). Since the early 1950s, work/life balance has been of interest to researchers across a variety of academic disciplines, including psychology, sociology, business, and public policy. This topic has, particularly in the last 20 years, become a hot topic for organizational leaders — especially HR leaders. In general, the research has been robust but academic in nature, and a strong business case is rarely made to justify an investment in work/life balance policies — beyond the "it's the right thing to do" approach.

What the Research Tells Us

Achieving a true "balance" between work and personal life is highly unlikely. With the proliferation of technology and 24/7 connectivity, the two roles are going to interact and intersect often. Most of the early research focused on work/life *conflict*, which refers to how employees manage conflict between the family role and work demands. Conflict often arises as a result of an incompatibility between individuals' work and family roles. When employees experience conflicting or incompatible pressures, pressure in one role (e.g., the family role) is made more difficult by pressure in the other (e.g., the work role).[1]

A myriad of explanations have been offered as to the reason conflict arises between work and family roles. Some have argued that conflict increases as the number of hours worked per week increases,[2] when employees perceive a lack of control over their work hours,[3] or when employees' schedules are unpredictable or irregular.[4] Others have suggested that work/life conflict increases when employees' work roles are ambiguously defined, or various work roles conflict with one another — not knowing what the job will look like from day to day.[5] Constant changes in the work environment, general work stress, and high demands on one's mental capacities have also been found to increase employees' work-family conflict.[6]

Other research describes work/life conflict as a "stressor" that can lead to a variety of symptoms, including anxiety, fatigue, depression, and burnout.[7] Many of the academics who look at the stressors and strain theories assume that work/life conflict only happens in one direction — when work conflicts with life. More likely, work/life conflict can work in either direction, such that work interferes with life as much as life interferes with work.[8]

All this researching and theorizing has really just shifted the emphasis from looking at work/life conflict to the more encompassing concept of work/life balance or flexibility. Despite the progress researchers have made in understanding the concept of work/life balance, the practical research is lacking. First, a need exists for more valid tools to measure work/life balance or satisfaction with work/life balance in organizations. Second, it remains unclear which specific resources or initiatives offered by organizations are actually helpful for work/life balance. For example, cognitive attributes such as creativity or behavioral attributes such as life management skills may enable some employees to better balance work and live and derive satisfaction from each domain.

In this chapter we attempt to present practical, field-tested approaches to work/life flexibility and outline the benefits of such programs in organizations. In addition, we present our business-focused approach to provide you with the tools necessary to build a business case for your work/life balance programs and to show their return on investment.

Effective Design and Execution

Companies that offer comprehensive work/life practices and policies are becoming increasingly attractive. A recent survey conducted by the Association of Executive Search Consultants (AESC), showed that 85 percent of recruiters have seen candidates reject a job offer based solely on work/life balance concerns. The vast majority of recruiters in the AESC study indicated that employees care more about work/life balance considerations now than they did just five years ago. In a recent study conducted by the Families and Work Institute, 87 percent of both high-wage (i.e., executive or management level) and lower wage (i.e., front-line staff) employees indicated that work/life flexibility was an extremely important factor in choosing a new job.[9] In response, two-thirds of companies are developing programs to help top candidates boost their family time without sacrificing their careers.[10]

Other researchers examined the work/life balance practices of the companies identified by *Fortune* magazine in 2009 as the "100 Best Companies to Work For."[11] They found that these companies use many innovative work/life balance programs, policies, and practices to differentiate themselves from their competitors. In particular, the practices discussed below were prevalent in nearly all the companies on *Fortune*'s list and were identified by the researchers as best practices in work/life balance. As a reminder, simply replicating these practices in your organization will not guarantee success. However, these practices and examples of the ways in which they have been implemented in other organizations may be informative as you prepare to build or enhance your own work/life balance program(s).

Support Family Responsibilities

SAS (an analytics software company) helps employees spend more time with their families by employing a standard 35-hour workweek. They also have four 4subsidized, onsite daycare programs to accommodate 850 children.

Principal Financial Group (a financial services company) offers a program entitled Working Caregiver Leave. Under this program, employees have the opportunity to work part time for up to 12 weeks per year, while maintaining full benefits and guaranteed job security.

Offer Programs Geared Toward Improving Employee Health

Quad/Graphics (a printing company) has offered onsite medical clinics since 1990.Nearly 80 percent of the company's employees use the onsite clinics as their main source of primary care and specialty care, including internal medicine, pediatrics, obstetrics, gynecology, and optometry.

Eileen Fisher (a designing and retail firm of women's fashion) offers complimentary onsite yoga, foot reflexology, and massage to all employees. The company also reimburses all employees up to $1,000 per year for wellness-related expenses.

Offer Paid Time Away From Work

Whole Foods Market (a natural and organic supermarket) offers a program in which employees are able to earn additional hours to be used toward paid time off.

Four Seasons Hotels (operator of luxury hotels and resorts) offers all employees who have been with the company for six months (including those in service-related jobs) the opportunity to stay three nights free at any Four Seasons property. After a year of employment, the number of free nights increases to six, and so on with tenure.

Support Employees in Pursuing Further Education and Training

A.G. Edwards (a financial services holding company) allows employees to earn up to 29 hours of undergraduate college credit for job-related classes, which are held onsite through the internal training department.

Google (an Internet services company) will reimburse employees up to $8,000 per year for work-related courses provided by external trainers or academic institutions. Through Google's Global Education Leave Program, workers can take up to five years of leave to further their education and be reimbursed up to $150,000 for educational expenses.[12]

Support Employees' Volunteer Efforts

America Online Inc. (an Internet services and media company) launched AOL Tech Corps, a group of America Online volunteers who assist nonprofit organizations with technology-related projects, such as upgrading their computer systems.

Ernst and Young (an accounting firm) started a Corporate Social Responsibility Fellows Program, through which employees can help organizations in developing countries.

Building Business-Focused Work/Life Balance Programs

Work/life balance and flexibility have gained a lot of popularity with consulting firms and organizations over the past few decades. Unfortunately, their growth in popularity has not coincided with a comparable growth in the known business value of these initiatives. They sound great; they sound like the right thing to do — but do they have any practical, bottom-line value to the organization? HR leaders tend to believe that positive outcomes result from implementing work/life balance initiatives — however, without proving their worth, they are just another HR "initiative of the month."

Work/life programs themselves are rarely inherently problematic; however, their execution is often hindered by a lack of executive-level support and an unclear linkage to meaningful business outcomes. By making such programs business-focused, HR leaders can more effectively achieve buy-in from critical stakeholders and ensure that the program is adding value to the business.

The key questions to ask and answer when implementing a business-focused, work/life balance program are as follows:

1. *Determine critical outcomes.* What outcomes/metrics are the senior leaders in this organization looking to improve by implementing work/life balance initiatives? These typically range from reduced turnover and stress to increased productivity and morale.

2. *Create a cross-functional data team.* Who owns the specific data/metrics on which senior leaders are focused? How do I connect with those individuals to obtain the data? Does human resources already own some of this data?

3. *Assess outcome measures.* Are the relevant business data/metrics collected at the appropriate level for me to make apples-to-apples comparisons (e.g., department level/district level)?

4. *Analyze the data.* Do I have the statistical capabilities in-house, or do I need to look at a university or consulting firm to help me analyze the data? Based on the analysis, have I built an effective business case that shows the impact of work/life balance on the critical business outcomes identified previously?

5. *Build the program and execute.* Based on the linkage analysis, and in talking with employees, what is the highest priority/ROI project? Where is the best place to pilot a work/life balance initiative?

6. *Measure and adjust.* How do I assess the change/impact that has occurred, demonstrate it to senior leaders, and make adjustments to maximize effectiveness?

Often, the employee opinion survey is a great place to start building the business case for work/life balance initiatives. An effective survey contains items that center around work/life balance issues. A sample item maybe: "My manager helps me balance my work/life responsibilities," or "My manager values the work/life balance initiatives in this organization," or even "I don't feel guilty when I leave work early to deal with a personal matter." Your first step in building the business case is to take the work/life balance items on your survey and link them to other "outcome" items on the survey — such as turnover intentions (for example, "I would stay with this organization if offered a similar job at another company") or the overall "morale" items on the survey. The data may show that stronger perceptions of work/life balance lead to lower turnover intentions and higher morale. Then, you can link the work/life balance items to your employees' individual performance data (if you capture that in your performance management tool) to demonstrate the connection between employees' perceptions of work/life balance and their on-the-job performance. Think about the difference such analyses can make when presenting a new work/life balance initiative to your senior leaders:

"We should do this because it is popular, and XYZ Consulting says we should do it."

versus

"We should do this because it will lead to better recruitment opportunities, lower turnover, higher engagement, and stronger employee productivity."

Remember, your goal in all this is not solely to improve your work/life balance score on your employee survey — *it is to positively impact business outcomes as well!*

You may be authorized to begin the journey by pilot-testing some work/life balance initiatives in certain areas of your organization. These initiatives may come in the form of flextime, rotating schedules, or telecommuting. No matter where you start with the pilot, make sure that you collect performance data from across the entire organization so that you can compare changes in business outcomes for those who participate with those who do not participate. Again, you are building a business case based on business outcomes, period. The results of the pilot test should not center solely on whether or not "the employees really liked it."

Case Study: UPS

For years, one of the most demanding jobs at UPS has been driver-supervisor. The leadership at UPS recognized this fact and were proactive in addressing the challenges of the position before driver-supervisors could experience burnout, become less effective as leaders, or leave the organization altogether. They tested different approaches to scheduling, such as flextime, and found that work units with work/life balance initiatives in place performed significantly better than those that did not have these initiatives.

UPS took it a step further and identified, using rigorous data analysis, that having only work/life balance initiatives was not enough — leaders had to *believe* in the initiatives. With that, they began to survey the driver-supervisors every quarter — focusing on the work/life culture in their specific work units. Further analyses showed that groups having work/life balance initiatives in place *and* a strong work/life balance culture outperformed all other work units in terms of increased productivity and reduced supervisor turnover. This business case continues to be validated with disciplined data collection and analytics.

This case study is enlightening because it focuses on the value of a work/life culture in the organization. The work/life culture is often ignored in organizations — but there can be some unwritten rules about taking advantage of work/life balance initiatives. First, employees may perceive that career options are limited for those individuals who use the programs. If the organization's culture does not support the work/life initiatives, then they will be underused, and their impact will be muted. Including items related to work/life balance on an annual survey and acting upon the results helps build a culture that supports work/life balance initiatives and sends the message that they are available for all employees to use.

The UPS example is all about the importance of buy-in. Imagine approaching front-line managers who have a full plate of responsibilities and asking them to work their people less, let them go home earlier, or let them work from home. This proposition would not likely go over well. Starting with attitude data, moving to pilot data, and then continuing with deeper data collection and analytics not only builds the business case but sustains it. Some obvious limitations need to be communicated regarding programs that can be implemented. For example, someone who is a delivery driver cannot work from home. Any types of limitations should be discussed transparently and directly with employees before expectations become raised (particularly if the concerns are cost related).

Practical Tips

Based on our experiences addressing work/life issues in organizations, we offer the following practical tips for developing and implementing business-focused, work/life balance programs:

- Build a true business case for creating a work/life balance program.
- Identify a real need and define the outcomes you expect from the investment.
- Do not be surprised when a senior leader is skeptical of making these types of investments. Anticipate such resistance and prepare reasonable, financially sound responses.
- When deploying a program, openly communicate the value, as well as the business justification and benefits, to leaders and employees.
- A good place to start understanding the potential benefits of a work/life program is your employee survey. A linkage analysis with business outcomes can help define the expected benefit of the program and make it business-focused.
- Continue to measure expected outcomes of time so that the ROI can be regularly calculated and communicated.
- Recognize that oftentimes specific work/life benefits are meaningful to some employees and not to others (for example, onsite daycare).
- Ensure new programs are focused on meeting a specific need in your organization.
- Front-line managers can either support or derail your efforts to implement these types of programs. Make sure you engage them and clearly communicate the value of program participation.
- Leverage the program to the fullest extent when recruiting and hiring employees. Doing so will help you attract top candidates and build a strong business case.
- Recognize the uniqueness of your organization's culture and give careful consideration to whether off-the-shelf programs effectively address your needs.

CHAPTER 12

Creating a Business-Focused HR Scorecard

Talking about human resource's lack of a "seat at the table" is common. This notable absence is typically due to limited hard data that demonstrate human resources' value and contributions. This book has shown you how to demonstrate that value across key processes. The final remaining piece of the puzzle that helps pull it all together is to track the key people drivers of the business on an HR scorecard. We will briefly review the research and best practices related to HR scorecards and then profile a sample scorecard focused on business outcomes.

What the Research Tells Us

Organization-wide balanced scorecards were introduced in the mid-1990s as a way of showing the connection between long-term strategy and short-term actions.[1] These scorecards not only include financial metrics but also metrics for customers, internal business processes, and employees, thus allowing senior team members to track performance and monitor the effect of business initiatives in these key areas. All the metrics on the organization-wide balanced scorecard are typically connected to business outcomes directly.

In addition to the organization-wide scorecard, most HR departments have begun to develop their own HR-focused metrics (i.e., the HR balanced scorecard). The HR scorecard sees HR management practices as a strategic asset and provides a road map to help organizations integrate HR systems with organizational strategy. In theory, the scorecard contains measures of past performance and drivers of future performance.[2]

Similar to the organizational scorecard, the HR balanced scorecard generally includes measures that capture four distinct perspectives: financial, operations, customer relations, and learning and growth.[3] The financial perspective refers to how human resources adds value to the company's bottom line (typically cost savings) by, for example, helping hire and retain high-performing employees. The operations perspective focuses on internal processes critical to ensuring fulfillment of both customers' needs and the organization's mission. Processes include staffing, technology, and many other

161

people-focused HR activities (e.g., performance management and succession planning). The customer perspective includes measures of how human resources meets and surpasses the needs of both internal and external customers. Finally, the learning and growth perspective focuses on training and people development processes, including onboarding and ongoing career development. Ideally, the inclusion of measures representing each of these four perspectives should help take the guesswork out of identifying the most important HR metrics.

Researchers also draw a distinction between lagging and leading indicators. Lagging indicators would be those that reflect only what has happened in the past. For example, financial metrics measure the impact of previous decisions. As the sources of such outcomes are not always clear, lagging indicators may often be inadequate in helping assess decisions in today's dynamic work environment. Leading indicators differ from organization to organization, but they assess the status of key drivers that lead to the success of the organization's strategy. Leading indicators stress the effect of future rather than past decisions and may include strategic, operations, and customer perspectives.[4]

Although organizations differ in the many ways to create a scorecard, to be most useful scorecards should include the four dimensions outlined in Table 12.1.

Table 12.1

HR Scorecard Element	Definition
Deliverables	The key HR deliverables that will help to leverage HR's role in your company's overall business strategy
Processes	The key HR processes (e.g., selection, performance management, compensation)
Alignment	Clear alignment between the HR deliverables/processes and the overarching business strategy
Results	An indicator of the effectiveness with which the deliverables are executed.

Effective Design and Execution

Researchers have identified a step-by-step process for designing and implementing an HR scorecard. Following the four steps in the order outlined below helps focus scorecard development efforts and secure thorough and successful execution.

1. *Planning and alignment.* During this stage, the project is defined. Plans, objectives, and timelines are established. Other actions taken during this stage include training on the balanced scorecard method, measures, and the impacts of the scorecard on the organization.

2. *Assessment.* This stage includes a critical examination of the current metrics used to evaluate HR effectiveness and the value of those measures to business strategy.

3. *Development.* This stage involves designing the HR measures to be included on the balanced scorecard. During the development stage, relevant criteria are identified, participants are established, the process for tracking performance and data collection is outlined, and an effective communication strategy is created.

4. *Implementation.* The final stage involves putting the HR scorecard into operation and initiating the ongoing evaluation of HR initiatives, including performance and value added to the business strategy. Implementation is a not a one-time measurement process. Data collection, analysis, and reporting should happen as opportunities arise. For example, employee survey data on the scorecard should be updated every time your organization conducts the survey, whereas hiring metrics could be updated monthly.

In addition to determining the above process, researchers have identified the critical factors that can contribute to the successful implementation of an HR scorecard and measurement system.[5]

- *Senior management champion.* Any organization-wide initiative that is expected to have a substantial and lasting effect needs to have support from senior management. The role of the champion is to ensure that the measurement processes are visible, credible, and a priority for the organization.

- *Accountability.* This factor revolves around the successful execution of the initiative. For example, human resources may be accountable for implementing a policy, practice, or procedure to achieve the result, whereas the line manager may have the accountability to execute the policy, practice, or procedure. When making the process business-focused, you will need to demonstrate the business impact of that policy, practice, or procedure (more on this later).

- *Validity.* Can the numbers be trusted? The HR scorecard must contain measures and metrics that are clearly understood by leaders inside and outside human resources and that have been closely examined for accuracy. If the numbers cannot be verified via key tracking mechanisms, such as an HRIS system, or if the credibility of the measures becomes questionable, then trust in the measurement system will break down.

- *Actionable.* For an HR scorecard to be meaningful, it must contain only those measures that are most essential to the HR strategy *and* to the strategic plan of the organization. In fact, a few vital measures provide greater insight and create better opportunities to take action than a list of marginally useful metrics.

- *Dynamic.* Things change. Forces outside our control require us to rethink our plans. In making the process business-focused, you will need to be disciplined to reanalyze your data and discover new drivers of business outcomes from an HR perspective. These new drivers will then need to be added to the scorecard.

■ *Distributed*. The HR scorecard must be communicated throughout the organization. Many of the initiatives will be carried out and implemented by managers and employees outside human resources.

Building the Business-Focused HR Scorecard

The research provides good, theoretical advice on how to build and implement HR scorecards in organizations. Unfortunately, HR leaders have taken a sharp detour in their quest to find the magic metrics they should measure.[6] Misguided metrics typically focus on HR efficiencies, such as time-to-hire or a staffing ratio. Efficiency metrics are solid ways to measure just that — efficiency. Cost-centers measure their effectiveness by showing greater efficiency. If human resources wants to be a business partner, it must show business impact. The approach we have applied to all the HR processes discussed in this book is also relevant to the development of an HR scorecard. The steps to take are straightforward, and if your HR processes are business-focused, then you only need to add the key business drivers from each of those processes to your scorecard and set goals around them.

Executives want to believe in the value of their employees, but they often struggle to understand how the HR function truly drives value through the organization's people. As HR thought leader Dave Ulrich stated:

> One of the most common weaknesses of HR professionals is fear of quantitative, measurable results. Such fears may come from lack of knowledge or experience with empirical assessments of HR work. It is clearly time to replace fear with resolve.[7]

So how has that resolve worked out for HR leaders? That quote is almost a decade-and-a-half old, and HR professionals still struggle to quantify their results. Typically, human resources will chip in with an employee engagement score, which as we discussed in Chapter 1 is not a business outcome. Alternatively, they may offer metrics around rates of turnover; however, these statistics tell us nothing about what is actually driving turnover. Creating sound metrics around the activities that human resources does to drive business outcomes will solidify *accountability* and give HR leaders an opportunity to reach the status of trusted advisor and to have a respected voice in the boardroom.

Let us start with the key steps that build upon what the researchers said and that will make the HR scorecard business-focused.

Every element on the scorecard must be directly linked to business outcomes. The "Analyze the Data" step from the Business Partner Roadmap™ is usually the step that trips up HR leaders. However, to be business-focused, this step is the most critical one for a scorecard. Remember, each organization is unique. What drives business outcomes on the people side in one organization may not drive business outcomes in another. Thus, analyzing *your* data and connecting it to business outcomes that matter in your organization is imperative. Human resources still does not have a standard set of agreed-upon metrics as, for example, does accounting. This, though, is not a bad thing for human resources because different people-focused initiatives will have different effects on business outcomes. Innovation may be a competency that is critical at Google; however, it may not matter as much for employees at the local power company.

The beauty of taking this customized, analytics-driven approach is that it will make you more credible. Imagine showing your HR scorecard to the senior team and being able to statistically demonstrate the cause-effect relationship to business outcomes and the return on investment (ROI) for each metric. Can you do that now? Some HR efficiency measures might be appropriate. For example, if you can prove that faster time-to-hire leads directly to better hires, then great — put it on the scorecard. Alternatively if you can prove that faster time-to-hire leads to poor hiring and that a slower, more structured process results in better hiring decisions, then put the latter process on the scorecard. Your HR balanced scorecard needs to contain metrics that hold your HR leaders accountable for the effective implementation of the initiatives that you have discovered drive your business outcomes.

What has typically been done in the past and what is done today is strikingly different. In the past, you may have identified "survey participation rate" and "days to fill a job" as key metrics. These are noteworthy, but are they connected in any way to improving the organization? Do we have any analytics behind them to "sell" them to front-line managers? Linking all elements of the HR scorecard to critical business outcomes helps attract buy-in from managers across all levels of the organization and to ensure the relevance and sustainability of your measurement processes.

If it is a significant driver of business outcomes, put it on the scorecard. If you have implemented an HR initiative, it is likely that it will touch all, or almost all, your workforce. Management at all levels wants to know if these initiatives are making a difference — the scorecard is a great way to communicate that impact. Creating metrics is as much about the numbers as it is about the buy-in and communication of the metrics. The outcomes of your analysis on each of the HR processes will reveal the type of metrics to include in the scorecard. For example, if participation in work/life flexibility programs contributes to lower turnover rates and increased productivity, then a goal around participation rates in this program would be a valuable metric to include on the scorecard. Training participation carries much more weight as a metric if it brings with it an explanation of how employee participation drives key business outcomes.

Communicate the value of the scorecard to senior and front-line leaders. In our experience working with front-line managers, a majority tend to be skeptical of HR initiatives and scorecards because they know that such initiatives equate to additional items on their to-do list. By walking front-line managers through the connections between what you are asking them to do and their business outcomes, you will gain the buy-in you are looking for.

Case Study: Product Shrink

The case study focuses on a retail organization that had been in operation for years. As a consequence of tough economic times and global marketplace competition, this organization was facing the prospect of substantially slowing their growth plans and possibly laying off numerous employees. Reducing costs across their entire network of stores was thus critical to maintaining their plans and sustaining their existing employment levels.

The key business outcome, as identified by leaders across multiple functions, was to increase profitability by reducing product shrink. Product shrink refers to employee and nonemployee theft of merchandise as well as loss of saleable product due to damage. Shrink had cost this organization hundreds of millions of dollars annually and impacted their bottom-line profits. Senior leaders turned to human resources for answers, thus providing HR leaders a chance to significantly impact a business outcome that was critical to the organization's survival.

During this critical time, saying that HR processes were "aligned" with the key business outcome was not enough. Rather, HR leaders had to demonstrate that their efforts had a cause-effect impact on the business outcome. Following our three key tenets above, first people data (e.g., employee opinion survey results, training participation rates, competency ratings, and hiring criteria) were statistically linked to product shrink. The key cause-effect drivers, which included competencies, attitudes, training, and even termination rates, are listed below (and depicted in Figure 12.1):

- *Achieve extraordinary results.* This driver came directly from the organization's competency model for front-line managers. The competencies on which managers were rated included employee development, leadership, decision-making ability, execution, and collaboration/teamwork.
- *Dishonesty terminations.* This driver was culled from the organization's database of employee turnover. The data represent the number of individuals at each store who were terminated for dishonesty (defined simply as product theft).

Figure 12.1

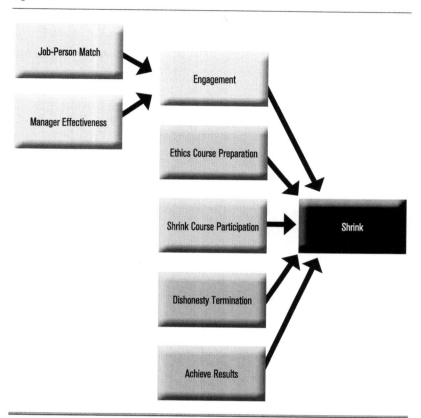

- *Ethics course participation.* This driver of product shrink came from the organization's learning management system (LMS) database, which collects participation rates on the company's training courses. The data showed the percentage of current employees who had completed this "mandatory" course. Higher participation in this course led to lower internal theft (a key component of product shrink).
- *Sales/shrink course participation.* The data regarding participation rates in this mandatory training, which also came from the organization's LMS database, showed the percentage of current employees who had completed this course. Much like the ethics course, higher participation in the sales/shrink course resulted in lower levels of product shrink.
- *External customer focus.* This driver was one of the dimensions measured on the organization's annual employee opinion survey. The importance of this survey

dimension was revealed after we conducted a factor analysis of the database used by the organization's survey vendor.

- *Job-person match*. This driver, which was one of the dimensions measured on the organization's annual employee opinion survey, was a sub-driver of product shrink. Although Job-Person Match was not a direct causal driver of shrink, it was a causal driver of Customer Focus, thus contributing indirectly to shrink. Job-Person Match was also an important dimension that was revealed after we conducted a factor analysis of the survey vendor's database.

As a result of this analysis, the drivers outlined in Figure 12.1 were added to the HR scorecard. For the first key driver —Achieve Extraordinary Results — the metric included on the scorecard was to increase the percentage of managers who received a rating of 4 or 5 on this competency from 10 percent currently to 25 percent. The organization set this metric with the knowledge that this managerial competency was directly linked to improved product shrink. The rationale behind the increase was that, based on the training and coaching initiatives to be implemented, managers' performance would increase and that such increases would be reflected in their competency ratings on their annual performance reviews. You may be thinking that these scores could easily have been manipulated by the senior manager (by rating his or her managers higher). This risk is always present, but a checks-and-balances process was in place to compare the managers' actual numbers with the previous year to see if they had truly "achieved outstanding results." This process reduced the temptation to inflate ratings for managers who had not truly achieved outstanding results.

The second key driver of product shrink was reducing Dishonesty Terminations. Annually, 10 percent of the organization's terminations were due to dishonesty. The metric established was to reduce dishonesty terminations to five percent for the year. The organization wanted to set an aggressive goal for this problem, as it represented a direct loss of goods and an instant hit on store profitability. Establishing a goal of 5 percent was not an exact science, but HR leaders believed it was a challenging yet realistic stretch goal that, if achieved, would contribute meaningfully to the overall reduction in product shrink. This goal was to be achieved by implementing several new selection instruments (for example, integrity tests and ethics courses). The regular monitoring of the store's product-shrink numbers, which reflected dishonesty (e.g., theft) in the workplace, provided the necessary checks and balances. HR leaders were able to obtain buy-in not only for the new metric but also for the new selection instruments because they could demonstrate the connection between the two and had provided front-line managers with an effective upstream weapon to battle dishonesty in their stores via a more effective hiring process.

The third key driver of product shrink was the percentage of all employees, at the store level, who had completed the organization's ethics and shrink training courses in the past year. At the time of this intervention, the organization had a completion rate of just 65 percent (these were "mandatory" courses!). This metric was set to reach a 95 percent completion rate for the year, and every year after that. All the organization's leaders were on-board with this new metric, due in part to their embarrassment at achieving only a 65 percent completion rate for mandatory courses. What had changed was that they no longer looked at these training courses as boxes to check when new employees were hired. The new attitude was that, to reduce product shrink and impact bottom-line results, these courses needed to be completed and retaken annually. Managers began to co-lead many of the sessions to emphasize key points and further drive down their product-shrink numbers.

The final key drivers of product shrink came from employee attitudes, specifically Job-Person Match and External Customer Focus. Rather than setting a metric that focused on overall employee satisfaction or engagement — which is a generic measure of employee attitudes — the metrics were set around a strong, significant improvement in these two key drivers of engagement. The metrics were set to reach a statistically significant improvement on all items that made up these two areas of employee attitudes.

Calculating Return on investment

In calculating the ROI of these key cause-effect drivers of shrink, we need to look at several essential pieces of information (see Table 12.2).

Table 12.2. Calculating Return-on-Investment

Intervention	Beta (Impact)	Potential Shrink Impact
Manager Competency	0.14	$13.0 million
Ethics Course	0.10	$9.3 million
Shrink Course	0.09	$8.4 million
Dishonesty Terminations	-0.08	$7.4 million
Engagement	0.04	$3.7 million
Reward & Recognition	ns	ns
Customer Satisfaction	ns	ns

At the time of our intervention, the organization was losing $93 million to annualized shrink. Based on this number and the impact scores provided in the table, we calculated the following:

Ethics Course Impact — currently 65 percent participation in Ethics Course

- Increasing participation to 95 percent could result in additional savings of $4.3 million
- Approximate cost of increasing ethics course participation was equal to $1,100,000 (employee time, communication)
- Expected ROI: 390 percent (which is the $1.1 million in cost divided by the $4.3 million in potential savings)

The same process was used to calculate the potential shrink impact for each of the other key drivers.

The key takeaways from this case study are listed below:

- The organization did not use some generic HR metrics. They used their data, linked it to their business outcomes, and determined, specifically, what they should invest in and what they should track on their HR scorecard.
- The organization calculated an ROI for each of the areas identified as drivers of product shrink and placed on the HR scorecard.
- The HR leaders communicated frequently to senior and front-line management about the research they had conducted and the bottom-line impact of their efforts. Buy-in was not a problem for this HR department.
- The organization beat their product shrink goals by 33 percent in the first year. The expectations are to sustain this level of performance but also, on an annual basis, to reanalyze the latest people and product shrink data as environmental factors change and ongoing improvements are made.

Practical Tips

- Every metric on the HR scorecard should either have an impact on business outcomes or actually be a business outcome (e.g. productivity).
- Share with front-line leaders the impact that your metrics have on business outcomes to get their buy-in.
- Efficiency metrics are not enough to show the value of human resources on the business.
- Find a senior manager who is not from human resources to champion the HR scorecard, thereby giving it greater credibility.
- Make the scorecard easy to read, and clearly show the ROI for each of the individual metrics tracked.
- Use advanced statistics (e.g., t-tests) to generate goals that are statistically significant.

CHAPTER 13

Bringing It All Together:
Next Steps and Opportunities

Our goals for the book were threefold. The first was to bring the academic and applied research to the forefront and break it down into practical terms for leaders in organizations. The second goal was to pull together the best practices in executing the HR processes showcased here. Finally, we aimed to make each of these processes business-focused by providing tips and tools for aligning the processes with business needs and demonstrating their value, impact, and the return on investment (ROI) for the organization. We have used practical terms and simplified the information to make it as actionable as possible for HR leaders. A deep disconnect between academic research and practical, everyday HR activities still remains. We doubt this book will put an end to that. However, it should provide you with an opportunity to make your HR function much more effective — as well as more focused on your organization's bottom lines.

The next steps are to get out and apply what is shown here — we know that is easier said than done — but the hard work and the outcomes you will create will be worth it. The case studies presented in this book are real; they took hard work and true commitment to making human resources better.

By implementing the 11 individual processes that drive business outcomes and by holding the HR function accountable with a well-designed scorecard focused on results, you can create sustainable impact and an HR strategy that will be directly aligned with the overall business strategy. In our first book, *Investing in What Matters*, we introduced ten guiding principles to drive HR strategy. They are worth revisiting here:

- Organizations already spend significant amounts of money on their people...they just don't spend it on the right things.
- Organizations make investments in people without any data or with the wrong data.
- People and organizations are complex. The linkages between attitudes and outcomes have to be understood within *your* organization using *your* data.
- The people data and outcome data do exist — you just have to go and get it.

- Once a connection is made with the data, accountability is unavoidable (and that's a good thing).
- Don't assume a link between employee data/processes and business outcomes — define this link and understand why or why not.
- Perceptions alone do not show up on the profit and loss statement.
- Use research to make better decisions — learn from the work of others.
- There is not a silver bullet — you still need to make these processes unique to your organization.
- Use analytics to build the business case for your solution and demonstrate the ROI after implementation; however; don't lose sight of the fact that your solutions need to be practical.[1]

If you can apply these tips in your day-to-day work, then you will be on your way to creating a business-focused HR function. To get started in building your HR strategy that is based on facts, data, and ROI, ask yourself this: where is your organization on the HR measurement continuum (see Figure 13.1)?

Figure 13.1 HR Measurement Continuum

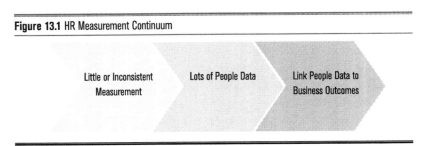

If you are on the left side with little or inconsistent measurement (as are many of the organizations we have worked with) — not a problem — you can start fresh and get it right from the beginning. The vast majority of organizations we work with fall in the middle category of having a lot of data that is stuck in many different areas of the organization. This indicates that more work is needed to obtain all the relevant data; however, once you have it, you can have a big impact on the bottom line. If you are on the far right of the continuum and have in-house expertise to link people data to business outcomes — then great! The key will be to apply this skill to focus on the short list of what drives the business and to employ this analytical capability in all your HR processes.

The opportunities are huge. Ensuring that HR processes are business-focused and are demonstrating their impact on bottom-line organization results will help the HR profession as a whole make great strides. Coveted "seat at the table" opportunities can be had when we, as HR professionals, quantify the impact of our actions and demonstrate our role as a valuable business partner.

APPENDIX A

Data Analytics

To the get the job done and to truly show the value and bottom-line impact of your people data, you will need to make some minor investments in statistical software, like the SPSS/AMOS program (www.spss.com).[1] This software gives you the ability to do some basic statistical analysis (means/averages and standard deviations) and somewhat more sophisticated analyses such as correlations and multiple regressions. These robust analyses can give you significant insights into your data. The AMOS program allows you to conduct the structural equation modeling (SEM) that is required to link multiple data sets together. Linking the multiple data sets is the key to showing the real impact in your organization. In addition, the AMOS program shows the causal relationships between your organization's people data and the critical outcomes that drive the business.

Personnel Specialists

We talked about a certain amount of "advanced statistical knowledge" being involved to conduct these analyses. However, before you think that you have to create an entire function full of Ph.D.s, take heart, the cost here will not be extreme. Sure, you will need to set up those cross-functional data teams (CFDTs) and have meetings and create presentations. But the actual analysis could be conducted by a professional statistician. However, for your organization, we do recommend a full-time Ph.D. in Industrial-Organizational (I/O) Psychology. Yes, a professional statistician will know how to do the structural equation modeling, but an I/O psychologist will have the requisite experience in not only statistics but also in people metrics/behaviors and business. This experience is relevant because once you discover how HR operations impact business outcomes, you will also want to have an individual who understands how to work on those important "operations."

The Society for Industrial and Organizational Psychology (SIOP) is a division of the American Psychological Association (APA) (Division 14) and is affiliated with the American Psychological Society (APS). We are not giving SIOP a free plug here. Instead, we are providing you with a resource to learn more about the skills and competencies of I-O psychologists. We hope you will call the authors of this book if you need help getting started, but just in case, the SIOP website (www.siop.org) has a "consultant locator" function to help you find a consultant and a "jobs" page if you would like to pursue full-time help. The SHRM website (www.shrm.org) also has this type of functionality.

Stakeholder Interview Guide

Before your initial cross-functional data meeting, conducting stakeholder interviews is essential. These interviews should involve you and all senior leaders (or senior leaders in your specific line of business). The goal of these interviews is to identify the truly critical outcomes the organization is aiming for. Second, within this context, the interviews will help these key stakeholders understand the potential invisible levers that can be pulled to enhance business outcomes. These interviews will provide both insights and buy-in for this considerable journey on which you are about to embark.

Rather than leave you on your own to build these interviews from scratch, we have provided (below) an effective template of key questions that should be asked during the stakeholder interviews that will elicit the information you will need to effectively launch and sustain your cross-functional data meetings.

Key Interview Questions

The following is a typical approach to introducing your goals for the interview with key stakeholders. You will, of course, need to customize this script for your organization as necessary:

> As your HR partner, we would like to more closely align our initiatives to your critical business outcomes. In order to do that we need to understand (1) how your business priorities, (2) what your related goals are, and (3) how they are measured. We then need to discover how HR initiatives and people data impact those business priorities. Our team will use advanced analytics to empirically connect the people data to the business data. In order to accomplish this, we will ask you and other senior leaders a series of structured questions. We ask for your support and input in gathering this information and in subsequent actions taken to impact your business priorities.

Business Priorities
- What are the strategic priorities of the organization?
- In your opinion, what are the most pressing issues facing this organization today? Are there issues facing particular segments of the business?
- What are your biggest barriers to overcome in addressing these issues/priorities?

Business Priorities — Goals and Measurement
- What measures/metrics are in place to show that progress is being made in these areas? What standards or goals have been set? How achievable are these goals?

People Priorities
- In your opinion, what are the most pressing issues facing the employee and customer population?
- How do these employee/customer issues impact business outcomes?

Business, Customer, and Employee Data
- Can you think of any key datasets that should be analyzed to discover causal drivers?
- Do you anticipate any barriers to obtaining the data needed from the various functions to conduct these analyses?
- Can you tell me anything else to ensure that the project will be successful?

Structure/Agenda of the Cross-Functional Data Team Meeting
When conducting the cross-functional data team meeting, quickly demonstrate not only the goal of meeting but also the value to the business that can be achieved by the participants. You will need to build a PowerPoint deck that articulates the following areas:
- Goal(s) of the Meeting
  - » Empirically link HR data to business-outcome data
  - » Prioritize HR strategy based on business impact
  - » Identify interventions and initiatives to drive the HR strategy
- Advantages/Positive Outcomes of Participation
  - » Provides additional levers to pull to impact functional outcomes
  - » Employs HR's assistance to help reach your function's goals
  - » Integrates data across functions to better align activities

- Discussion of Linkage-Analysis Methodology
  - » Allows for examining multiple data sets and outcomes simultaneously
  - » Offers a higher level of sophistication beyond correlation and regression
  - » Offers the ability to infer causality and strength of impact
- Strategic Initiative Review
  - » Summarize stakeholder interviews
  - » Agree on prioritization of stakeholder recommendations
- Balanced Scorecard Review
  - » Review how current priorities are measured today
- Critical Functional Metrics/Data Needs
  - » Based on priorities, discuss how data is measured for each area
  - » Identify data owners and sources for each function
- Next Steps
  - » Prioritize projects
  - » Set timelines and accountabilities
  - » Schedule follow-up meetings

The Concept of Causality

Throughout this book, we have discussed how to determine the "key causal drivers" of business outcomes. This is certainly a departure from various texts that show correlations between what the HR department does and certain bottom-line indicators. Our goal at this point is not to get into an overly detailed discussion of statistical analysis; however, we will discuss how we arrive at the phrase "key causal driver" and why you, the audience, need to grasp this concept.

First, let us cover some of the academic aspects of this analysis.

- *Theory.* In regard to academic research, a critical step to determining if data is truly causal is that they must be based on solid theory. In an academic setting, this would typically mean citing a previously conducted study that shows some sort of statistical connection between similar data to what you would be looking at. This standard is absolutely strong, whether it is from an academic or from a practitioner's perspective. If two variables (i.e., pieces of data) are linked together, they need to make intuitive sense or have some foundation in logical thought. We always propose that the models and analyses you run are done in what is called confirmatory mode, which means that you set up how the data should look before analyzing it, with the goal of confirming what you think should happen (i.e., your theory). The other mode of analysis is exploratory, which is where you throw the data into your statistical software and see where the data fall. Yes, you may make some interesting discoveries; however, if what is discovered is not based on logical reasoning or "theory," then you should never use the term "causal." For example, you may find that retail stores with higher turnover also have higher 401(k) plan participation. That is nice to know, but it makes little practical sense to start firing people so that you will have more people in the 401(k) plan.

- *Correlation.* In a similar fashion, what we have proposed throughout this book is not a correlational analysis. Correlations are useful when looking for a connection between two pieces of data. Correlations will only tell you whether or not one variable's strength is associated with another variable's strength (or weakness to weakness). This analysis can show you the strength of the relationship, and if the relationship is statistically significant. Correlations, however, do not demonstrate any type of causality whatsoever. The classic example of this fact is the connection between shark attacks and ice cream sales. We can truly find no logical reason for these two aspects of life to be connected, but they just happen to be connected. Both occur with more frequency in the summer months, an observation called a spurious correlation. From a practical perspective, such spurious correlations have the potential to misinform action and hinder improvement efforts.

- *Including all relevant causal variables.* Another key issue in determining whether a variable is causing another variable to happen is that you have included in that analysis all relevant causal variables. To clarify, you do not include only the variable that you hope is causing the business outcome but rather all the data that could possibly (based on logic, as discussed above) be a cause of the business outcome. In the grand scheme of things, including every possible cause of a business outcome is humanly impossible. However, both academically and practically, if you include all the data measured (and start measuring some key aspects that you have not measured in the past), you can make a strong inference and conclusion that a variable is a key causal driver of an outcome. This analysis will pass muster in the boardroom and at even the most discerning peer-reviewed academic journal. The point is that you must make a strong, good-faith effort to measure all that you can and include all of those measurements when you conduct the analyses.

- *Accounting for measurement error.* When you discuss with your team why you should use structural equation modeling versus less complex analytical techniques such as correlation or even multiple regressions, a key argument to make is that you will be able to account for measurement error. This benefit is a principal piece of information to have when you think about this analysis. With correlation and regression, which are strong analytical techniques, a chief assumption is that all data have been collected without any error. All data collected, particularly attitude data, performance ratings, or ratings of behavior, have error associated with their measurement. Whether it was the bad weather the morning of the survey, the cold coffee, the systematic error associated with the validity of the survey items, or the rating scales in the online performance-appraisal tool, that measurement contains some error. Structural equation modeling gives you a purer approach to the analysis because you get to account for that error in the analytics. That means there is one less assumption you have to make about the data you are analyzing. Does this mean that you can automatically claim causality? No. But it does get you one step further, and if you incorporate the previous three steps, you can begin to make such inferences of causality.

As we have mentioned throughout the book, we did not want to write a statistics textbook, and thankfully we have not. This appendix, and the next one, is designed to give you some of the ammunition you will need in the boardroom when you are asked questions about the process. Or when a senior executive realizes that you just asked for a large sum of money for an important project that is based on these types of analyses. Those senior leaders are just doing their due diligence (which they should), but you need to be able to show them that you have also done your due diligence.

Reliability and Validity

You will want to assess (or inquire about from a vendor) key areas of reliability and validity when implementing new HR tools or processes, particularly selection tests, employee surveys, and multi-rater assessments. Although you do not necessarily need to be an expert on the types of validity and reliability, you do need to be an educated consumer and should expect your vendors/partners to provide adequate evidence of the following topics.

Content Validity. Basing the items included in the instrument on a valid competency model with input from various leaders from across the organization will help you create a process that covers the critical aspects of the job. If you do not already have a competency model for key roles, then building out a competency model (see Chapter 5) is critical before building/executing other HR processes (e.g., multi-rater/360 assessments).

Discriminant Validity. As each role in the organization has multiple competencies, the HR tools must be able to assess each of these competencies uniquely. Put another way, the items in the measurement instrument must distinctly assess each element of, for example, "Relationship-Building" from "Holding Others Accountable." Discriminant validity is assessed by conducting an exploratory factor analysis to ensure that the items used to measure a specific competency are actually "hanging together" and are not overlapping or intercorrelating with other competencies.

Criterion-Related Validity. Arguably the most important aspect of validity, this analysis will assess whether the measures obtained using your HR tool are actually correlated with performance outcomes. To conduct this analysis, just attach a performance score(s) to each participants' multi-rater/360 scores and conduct a correlation. The outcome is referred to as a validity coefficient and will let you know if what is being assessed on the instrument is significantly related to actual individual performance.

Reliability. Numerous forms of reliability can be assessed; however, the most practical approach is to assess internal reliability. Using statistical software (for example, SPSS), you can calculate what is called coefficient alpha for each HR measure, which will let you know the level of consistency in the items on the instrument.

The rule of thumb is to have an alpha of at least 0.80 to be considered a reliable instrument.

Incorporating all of these validity and reliability assessments is critical on three fronts: scientific, legal, and practical. From a scientific perspective, having a valid and reliable instrument will ensure stable ratings that can be trusted to measure what they are supposed to be measuring. From a legal perspective, doing your due diligence on the front end of this process will only make you more bullet-proof if any objections are made as to how the data are or were used or how the assessments impacted individuals within the organization. From a practical standpoint, having a valid and reliable instrument built on a foundation of competencies that were conceived by various members of the organization and that are truly reflective of what is needed to perform the job will enhance the credibility of the instrument in the eyes of senior leaders and participants (i.e., the face validity). This, in turn, will increase senior-leader buy-in and help ensure that the results are taken seriously and are acted upon.

Endnotes

Preface

1. Mondore, S., and Douthitt, S. (2009). *Investing in what matters: Linking employees to business outcomes*. Alexandria, VA: Society for Human Resource Management.

Chapter 1

1. Cober, R., Silzer, R., & Erickson, A. (2009). Science-practice gaps in industrial-organizational psychology: Part I: Member data and perspectives, *The Industrial-Organizational Psychologist, 41*(1), 97-105.

2. Latham, G. (2009). *Becoming the evidence-based manager: Making the science of management work for you*. Boston, MA: Davies Black/Society for Human Resource Management.

3. Mondore, S., & Douthitt, S. (2009). *Investing in what matters: Linking employees to business outcomes*. Alexandria, VA: Society for Human Resource Management.

Chapter 2

1. Schmidt, F. L., & Hunter, J. E. (1998). The validity and utility of selection methods in personnel psychology: Practical and theoretical implications of 85 years of research findings. *Psychological Bulletin, 124*, 262-274.

2. Any staffing policies and approaches that HR considers should be thoroughly reviewed by legal counsel prior to implementation. See the Uniform Guidelines on Employee Selection Procedures (www.uniformguidelines.com) for more information.

3. Guion, R. M. (1998) *Assessment, measurement, and prediction for personnel decisions*. Mahwah, NJ: Erlbaum.

4. It should be noted that the legalities of pre-employment tests, including how they relate to the Americans with Disabilities Act (ADA), bona fide occupational qualifications (BFOQs), and drug testing, need to be of paramount

concern for employers, staffing professionals, and hiring managers. Discussion of these issues, however, is beyond the goals of this book. For a discussion of bona fide occupational qualifications (BFOQs), see Rhodes, R. A. (2002, March). Legal discrimination in four letters: BFOQ. *Connecticut Employment Law Letter.* Retrieved from www.halloran-sage.com/Knowledge /articleDetail.aspx?storyid=2055. For the most recent, hiring-related information regarding Americans with Disabilities, visit www.ada.gov. Finally, for more information on pre-employment drug screening, please visit www.employment-drugtesting.com/screening.html.

5. In our experience, outside consultants can offer numerous options for pre-employment tests, ranging from standard, off-the-shelf approaches that include tests of generalized competencies, skills, and abilities to completely customizable tests that can be tailored to specific competencies in the organization. Implementing validated tests is very cost-effective for HR leaders, as doing so will allow you to avoid the excessive time and expense of validating new pre-employment tests and can protect your organization from the risk of possible litigation that comes with using nonvalidated tests. In addition, sophisticated tracking mechanisms that allow the employer to track candidates throughout the hiring process are offered by many vendors. Nearly all pre-employment tests (outside of physical ability tests) are offered online, so the ease of use has increased substantially in recent years.

6. Barrick, M., & Mount, M. (1991). The big five personality dimensions and job performance: A meta-analysis. *Personnel Psychology, 44*(1), 1-26.

7. Many vendors use different terminology for different traits. Irrespective of terminology, these traits have a tremendous amount of overlap. When choosing a vendor, have the company provide the validity studies that show how well the traits that they assess predict future job performance. Also, be sure to note the extensiveness of the vendor's benchmark data (that is, norms), as this will give you a much better idea of the ranges of scores that represent a good fit for a particular job.

8. Reeve, C. L. (2007).Cognitive abilities. In S. G. Rogelberg (Ed.), *Encyclopedia of industrial and organizational psychology* (Vol. 1, pp. 76-79). Thousand Oaks, CA: Sage.

9. As defined in the Uniform Guidelines, adverse impact refers to a substantially different rate of selection in hiring, promotion, or other employment decision that disadvantages members of a particular race, sex, or ethnic group. Specifically, adverse impact is defined as a selection rate for any race, sex, or ethnic group that is less than four-fifths (or 80 percent) of the rate for the group with the highest rate. For additional information see the Uniform Guidelines on

Employee Selection Procedures, available at www.uniformguidelines.com/uniformguidelines.html.

10. 1Ployhart, R. E., & Holtz, B. C. (2008). The diversity-validity dilemma: Strategies for reducing racioethnic and sex subgroup differences and adverse impact in selection. *Personnel Psychology, 61*, 153-172.

11. Krause, D. E., Kersting, M., Heggestad, E. D., & Thornton, G. C. III. (2006). Incremental validity of assessment center ratings over cognitive ability tests: A study at the executive management level. *International Journal of Selection and Assessment, 14*, 360-371.

12. "Fact Sheet on Employment Tests and Selection Procedures," *The U.S. Equal Employment Opportunity Commission*, last modified on September 23, 2010. Available at www.eeoc.gov/policy/docs/factemployment_procedures.html.

13. Sackett, P. R., Schmitt, N., Ellingson, J. E., & Kabin, M. B. (2001). High-stakes testing in employment, credentialing, and higher education: Prospects in a post-affirmative action world. *American Psychologist, 56*, 302-318.

14. Wells, S. J. (2005). Diving in. *HR Magazine, 50*, 54-59.

15. Schmidt, F. L., & Hunter, J. E. (1998).

Chapter 3

1. Shippmann, J. S., Ash, R. A., Battista, M., Carr, L., Eyde, L. D., Hesketh, B., et al. (2000).The practice of competency modeling. *Personnel Psychology, 53(3)*, 703-740.

2. Zenger, J. H., & Folkman, J. (2002). *The extraordinary leader: Turning good managers into great leaders.* New York, NY: McGraw Hill.

3. Markus, L. H., Cooper-Thomas, H. D., & Allpress, K. N. (2005). Confounded by competencies? An evaluation of the evolution and use of competency models. *New Zealand Journal of Psychology, 34(2)*, 117-126.

4. Durgin, T. V. (2006). *Using competency management to drive organizational performance.* Washington, DC: Human Capital Institute.

5. Zenger, J. H., & Folkman, J. (2002).

6. The U.S. Department of Labor sponsors a website called Career One Stop, which contains an entire section devoted to educating consumers on the basics of competency models. It is basically a clearinghouse of previously created competency models and tips on creating your own.

7. These dictionaries typically provide definitions and observable behaviors that indicate the presence and level of a competency and denote which competencies have been used in the past in various industries and functions.

8. Markus et al. (2005).

Chapter 4

1. Campbell, J. P. (1990).Modeling the performance prediction problem in industrial and organizational psychology. In H. C. Triandis, M. Dunnette, & L. M. Hough (Eds.), *Handbook of industrial and organizational psychology* (2nd ed., Vol. 1, pp. 657-731). Palo Alto, CA: Consulting Psychologist Press.

2. Viswesvaran, C., & Ones, D. (2000).Perspectives on models of job performance. *International Journal of Selection and Assessment, 8*(4), 216-226.

3. Kingstrom, P. O., & Bass, A. R. (1981). A critical analysis of studies comparing behaviorally anchored rating scales (BARS) and other rating formats. *Personnel Psychology, 34,* 263-289.

4. For interested readers, the following sources provide a wealth of information about rating distortions during the performance appraisal process: MacMillan, A. (2006, April). Raising the bar on performance management: Best practices to optimize performance reviews and goal management. HR.com. Retrieved from www.hr.com; Murphy, K. R., & Cleveland, J. N. (1995). *Understanding performance appraisal: Social, organizational, and goal-based perspectives.* Thousand Oaks, CA: Sage; Pulakos, E. D. (2004). *Performance management: A roadmap for developing, implementing and evaluating performance management systems.* Alexandria, VA: Society for Human Resource Management.

5. Buchner, T. W. (2007). Performance management theory: A look from the performer's perspective with implications for HRD. *Human Resources Development International, 10*(1), 59-73.

6. Folan, P., & Brown, J. (2005). A review of performance measurement: Towards performance management. *Computers in Industry, 56,* 663-680.

7. Lautsch, B. A., Kossek, E. E., & Eaton, S. C. (2009).Supervisory approaches and paradoxes in managing telecommuting implementation. *Human Relations, 62*(6), 795-827.

Chapter 5

1. Brutus, S., London, M., & Martineau, J. (1999). The impact of 360-degree feedback on planning for career development. *Journal of Management Development, 18,* 676-693.

2. Bracken, D. W., Timmereck, C. W., & Church, A. H. (2001). *The handbook of multisource feedback.* San Francisco: Jossey-Bass.

3. Current practices in 360-degree feedback: A benchmark study of North American companies (2009, January). 3D Group. Retrieved from www.3dgroup. net/pr-012809.html.

4. Fleenor, J. W., Smither, J. W., Atwater, L. E., Braddy, P. W., & Sturm, R. E. (2010). Self-other rating agreement in leadership: A review. *Leadership Quarterly, 21*, 1005-1034.

5. Fleenor, J. W., Taylor, S., & Chappelow, C. (2008). *Leveraging the impact of 360-degree feedback*. San Francisco, CA: Pfeiffer.

6. Galbraith, J. R. (2009). *Designing matrix organizations that actually work: How IBM, Proctor & Gamble, and others design for success*. San Francisco, CA: Wiley.

7. Wimer, S. (2002). The dark side of 360-degree feedback: The popular HR intervention has an ugly side. *Training and Development*. Retrieved from www. star360feedback.com/old-site/360_article_dark_side.pdf.

8. Reichard, R. J., & Johnson, S. K. (2011).Leader self-development as organizational strategy. *Leadership Quarterly*, 22(1), 33-42.

9. Nowack, K., Hartley, G., & Bradley, W. (1999).Evaluating results of your 360-degree feedback intervention. *Training and Development, 53*, 48-53.

10. Brackan, D. W., & Timmereck, C. W. (2001); Lepsinger, R., & Lucia, A. D. (2009). *The art and science of 360 degree feedback*. San Francisco, CA: Jossey-Bass.

11. Chartered Management Institute. (2006). Using 360 degree feedback. Retrieved from www.star360feedback.com/old-site/360_degree_feedback_ using_360_degree_feedback.html.

12. Fleenor, J. W., Taylor, S., & Chappelow, C. (2008).

13. Heslin, P. A., Carson, J. B., & VandeWalle, D. (2009).Practical applications of goal-setting theory to performance management. In J. W. Smither & M. London (Eds.), *Performance management: Putting research into action* (pp. 89-116). San Francisco, CA: Jossey Bass.

14. MacMillan, A. (2006, April).Raising the bar on performance management: Best practices to optimize performance reviews and goal management. HR.com. Retrieved from www.hr.com.

15. Fleenor, J. W., Taylor, S., & Chappelow, C. (2008).

16. Lepsinger, R., & Lucia, A. D. (2009). *The art and science of 360 degree feedback*. an Francisco, CA: Jossey-Bass.

17. DeNisi, A. S., & Kluger, A. N. (2000). Feedback effectiveness: can 360-degree appraisals be improved? *Academy of Management Executive, 14*, 129-139.

18. Fleenor, J. W., Smither, J. W., Atwater, L. E., Braddy, P. W., & Sturm, R. E. (2010).

19. Maylett, T. (2009). 360-degree feedback revisited: The transition from development to appraisal. *Compensation Benefits and Review*. Retrieved from www.decision-wise.com/pdf/

Compensation-and-Benefits-Review-360-Degree-Feedback-Revisited-The-Transition-from-Development-to-Appraisal.pdf.

20. DeNisi, A. S. & Kluger, A. N. (2000).

21. Cascio, W., & Boudreau, J. (2008). *Investing in people: Financial impact of human resource initiatives.* Upper Saddle River, NJ: Pearson Education/Society for Human Resource Management.

Chapter 6

1. Kraut, A. (2006). *Getting action from organizational surveys.* San Francisco, CA: Jossey-Bass.

2. Podsakoff, N. P., Whiting, S. W., Podsakoff, P. M., & Blume, B. D. (2009). Individual- and organizational-level consequences of organizational citizenship behaviors: A meta-analysis. *Journal of Applied Psychology, 94,* 122-141.

3. Verheyen, L. G. (1998). How to develop an employee attitude survey. *Training & Management Journal, 42*(8), 72-76.

4. Bracken-Paul, K., & Bracken, D. W. (1995, January). Everything you always wanted to know about employee surveys. *Training and Development, 49*(1), 45-50.

5. Verheyen, L. G. (1998).

6. Visser, P. S., Krosnick, J. A., & Lavarkas, P. (2000). Survey research. In H. T. Reis & C. M. Judd (Eds.), *Handbook of research methods in social and personality psychology* (pp. 223-252). New York: Cambridge University Press.

7. Krosnick, J.A. (2002). The causes of no-opinion responses to attitude measures in surveys: They rarely are what they appear to be. In R. M. Groves, D. A. Dillman, J. L. Eltinge, & R. J. A. Little (Eds.), *Survey nonresponse* (pp.88-100). New York, NY: Wiley.

8. The University of Connecticut offers an easy-to-use sample size calculator, which can be accessed for free at www.gifted.uconn.edu/siegle/research/Samples/samplecalculator.htm.

9. Bracken-Paul, K., & Bracken, D. W. (1995).

10. Kaplan, R. S., & Norton, D. P. (1996). *The balanced scorecard: Translating strategy into action.* Boston, MA: Harvard Business Press.

11. Scott Ginnetti (personal communication, March 2010).

12. Dennis Wade (personal communication, January 2011).

Chapter 7

1. Goldstein, I. L., & Ford, K. J. (2002) *Training in organizations: Needs assessment development and evaluation.* Belmont, CA: Wadsworth Thomson Learning.

2. A more formal definition is that training is the systematic transfer of skills, concepts, or attitudes that results in improved performance in another environment.

3. Knowles, M. S. (1990) *The Adult Learner. A neglected species.* Houston, TX: Gulf.

4. Salas, E., & Cannon-Bowers, J. A. (2001). The science of training: A decade of progress. *Annual Review of Psychology, 52,* 471-499.

5. Sitzmann, T., Kraiger, K., Stewart, D., & Wisher, R. (2006). The comparative effectiveness of web-based and classroom instruction: A meta-analysis. *Personnel Psychology, 59,* 623-664.

6. Kirkpatrick, D. L. (1998). *Evaluating training programs: The four levels.* San Francisco, CA: Berrett-Koehler.

7. Salas, E., & Cannon-Bowers, J. A. (2001).

8. Dweck C. S. (2000).*Self-theories: Their role in motivation, personality, and development.* Philadelphia, PA: Psychology Press.

9. Kozlowski, S. W. J., Gully, S. M., Brown, K. G., Salas, E., Smith, E. A., & Nason, E. R. (2001). Effects of training goals and goal orientation traits on multi-dimensional training outcomes and performance adaptability. *Organizational Behavior and Human Decision Processes, 85,* 1-31.

Chapter 8

1. McDonald, K. S., & Hite, L. M. (2005).Reviving the relevance of career development in human resource development. *Human Resource Development Review, 4*(4), 418-439.

2. Yost, L. (2008, February). Managing across the generations: Knowing what motivates employees to excel is the key to effectively managing the multi-generational workplace. *BusinessNet.* Retrieved from http://findarticles.com/p/articles/mi_m1145/is_2_43/ai_n53301613.

3. Cummings, T. G., & Worley, C. G. (2005). *Organization Development and Change.* Cincinnati, Ohio: South-Western College.

4. Prince, J. B. (2003) Career opportunity and organizational attachment in a blue-collar unionized environment. *Journal of Vocational Behavior, 63,* 136-150.

5. Nayar, V. (2010). *Employees first, customers second: Turning conventional management upside down*. Boston, MA: Harvard Business Press.

6. Cummings, T. G., & Worley, C. G. (2005).

7. Baruch, Y. (2004). Transforming careers: From linear to multidirectional career paths. *Career Development International, 9*(1), 58-73.

8. Boen, J. L. (2009, March). Getting older but working longer: The average age at retirement is rising as nest eggs take a nosedive. *News-Sentinel.com*. Retrieved from www.news-sentinel.com/apps/pbcs.dll/article?AID=/20090330/NEWS /903300299.

9. Baruch, Y. (2004).

10. McDonald, K. S., & Hite, L. M. (2005).Reviving the relevance of career development in human resource development. *Human Resource Development Review, 4*(4), 418-439.

11. McDonald, K. S., & Hite, L. M. (2005).

12. Gentry, W. A., Griggs, T. L., Deal, J. J., & Mondore, S. P., (2009). Generational differences in attitudes, beliefs, and preferences about development and learning at work. In S. G. Baugh & S. E. Sullivan (Eds.), *Maintaining focus, energy, and options over the career*. Charlotte, NC: Information Age.

13. A half-day facilitated workshop with appropriate subject matter experts will usually suffice. Existing documents and tools (for example, competency models) should be leveraged, when possible, to develop an appropriate self-assessment framework.

Chapter 9

1. Day, D. V. (2000). Leadership development: A review in context. *The Leadership Quarterly, 11*, 581-613.

2. Lockwood, N. R. (2006). Leadership development: Optimizing human capital for business success. *SHRM Research Quarterly*. Retrieved from www.shrm. org/Research/Articles/Documents/1206RQuartpdf.pdf.

3. VanVelsor, E., & McCauley, C. D. (2004).Our view of leadership development. In C. D. McCauley& E. VanVelsor (Eds.), *The center for creative leadership handbook of leadership development* (pp. 1-22). San Francisco, CA: Jossey-Bass.

4. Day, D. V. (2007).Developing leadership talent: A guide to succession planning and leadership development. *Effective Practice Guidelines Series* (pp. 1-57). Alexandria, VA: Society for Human Resource Management Foundation.

5. McCall, M. W. (2010).Recasting leadership development. *Industrial and Organizational Psychology, 3*, 3-19.

6. SHRM Learning System (2009). Alexandria, VA: Society for Human Resource Management.

7. Kirkpatrick, D. L. (1998). *Evaluating training programs: The four levels.* San Francisco, CA: Berrett-Koehler.

8. Kilburg, R. R. (1996).Toward a conceptual understanding and definition of executive coaching. *Consulting Psychology Journal: Practice and Research, 48*(2), 134-144.

9. Feldman, D. C. (2001). Career coaching: What HR professionals and managers need to know. *Human Resource Planning, 24,* 26-35; Peltier, B. (2001). *The psychology of executive coaching.* New York, NY: Brunner-Routledge.

10. Bolch, M. (2001) Proactive coaching. Training, 38(5), 58-66; Gale, J., Liljenstrand, A., Pardieu, J., & Nebeker, D. M. (2002). Coaching: who, what, where, when and how. *Coaching World,* 93. Retrieved from www.coachfederation.org/includes/docs/004CoachingPracticesStudyGaleMar02.pdf.

11. Thach, E. (2002). The impact of executive coaching and 360 feedback on leadership effectiveness. *The Leadership & Organization Development Journal, 23*(4), 205-214.

12. Smither, J. W., London, M., Flautt, R., Vargas, Y., & Kucine, I. (2003). Can working with an executive coach improve multisource feedback ratings over time? A quasi-experimental field study. *Personnel Psychology, 56,* 23-44.

13. This approach is based on the assumption from adult learning theory that people learn most effectively when working on organizational problems in real time.

Chapter 10

1. Saba, J., & Martin, K. (2008, October). *Succession management: Addressing the leadership development challenge.* Boston, MA: Aberdeen Group; Succession Planning Training for Supervisors (2008). Alexandria, VA: Society for Human Resource Management.

2. Caudron, S. (2001, December). How HR drives profits. *Workforce Management, 80*(12), 16-31.

3. Huselid, M. A., Jackson, S. E., & Schuler, R. S. (1997).Technical and strategic human resource management effectiveness as determinants of firm performance. *Academy of Management Journal, 40,* 171-188.

4. Saba, J., & Martin, K. (2008).

5. *Succession Planning Training for Supervisors* (2008).

6. Charam, R. (2000, Summer). How to lower the risk in CEO succession. *Leader to Leader, 17.* Retrieved from www.pfdf.org/knowledgecenter/journal. aspx?ArticleID=21.

7. Wei, S., & Cannella, A. Jr. (2002).Power dynamics within top management and their impacts on CEO dismissal followed by inside succession. *Academy of Management Journal, 45,* 1195-1206.

8. Saba, J., & Martin, K. (2008).

9. Guthridge, M., Komm, A. B., & Lawson, E. (2006, February).The people problem in talent management. *McKinsey Quarterly, 2,* 6-8.

10. Byrne, J. A. (1998). How Jack Welch runs GE. *Business Week.* Retrieved from www.businessweek.com/1998/23/b3581001.htm.

Chapter 11

1. Greenhaus, J., & Beutell, N. (1985).Sources of conflict between work and family roles, *Academy of Management Review, 10,* 76-88.

2. Burke. R. J., Weir, T., & Duwors. R. E. (1980). Work demands on administrators and spouse well-being. *Human Relations, 33,* 253-278.

3. Valcour, M. (2007).Work-based resources as moderators of the relationship between work hours and satisfaction with work-family balance. *Journal of Applied Psychology, 92*(6), 1512-1523.

4. Pleck, J. H., Staines, G. L., & Lang. L. (1980).Conflicts between work and family life. *Monthly Labor Review, 103*(3), 29-32.

5. Kossek, E. E., & Ozeki, C. (1998). Work-family conflict, policies, and the job-life satisfaction relationship: A review and directions for future organizational behavior/human resources research. *Journal of Applied Psychology, 83,* 139-149.

6. Allen, T., Herst, D., Bruck, C., & Sutton, M. (2000). Consequences associated with work-to-family conflict: A review and agenda for future research. *Journal of Occupational Health Psychology, 5,* 278-308.

7. Latack, J. C. (1989). Work, stress, and careers: A preventive approach to maintaining organizational health. In M. B. Arthur, D. T. Hall, & B. S. Lawrence (Eds.), *Handbook of career theory* (pp. 252-274). Cambridge, England: Cambridge University Press.

8. Frone, M. R., Russell, M., & Cooper, M. L. (1995). Job stressors, job involvement and employee health: A test of identity theory. *Journal of Occupational and Organizational Psychology, 68*(1), 1-11.

9. Bond, J. T., & Galinsky, E. (2008).Workplace flexibility and low-wage employ-
    ees. *Families and Work Institute.* Retrieved from http://familiesandwork.org/
    site/research/reports/WorkFlexAndLowWageEmployees.pdf.

10. Ridge, B. (2007). Balance: The new workplace perk. *Forbes.com.*
    Retrieved from http://finance.yahoo.com/career-work/article/102685/
    Balance:-The-New-Workplace-Perk.

11. Bourne, K. A., Wilson, F., Lester, S. W., & Kickul, J. (2009).Embracing the
    whole individual: Advantages of a dual-centric perspective of work and life.
    Business Horizons, 52, 387-398.

12. While further education and training programs are a nice benefit for employ-
    ees, this example also illustrates where the definition of "work/life balance"
    seems to be stretched beyond its core meaning. If you ask yourself, "How does
    paying for an employee's education increase his or her work/life balance?" the
    answer is not obvious. In fact one could argue that working, fulfilling family
    responsibilities, and continuing one's education may actually increase stress.
    Nevertheless, the point of these programs is for an organization to support
    the educational endeavors of its employees if and when employees choose to
    continue their education.

Chapter 12

1. Kaplan, R. S., & Norton, D. P. (1996). *The balanced scorecard: Translating
    strategy into action.* Boston, MA: Harvard Business Press.

2. Becker, B. E, Huselid, M.A, & Ulrich, D. (2001). *The HR Scorecard: Linking
    people, strategy and performance.* Boston, MA: Harvard Business School Press.

3. Kaplan, R. S., & Norton, D. P. (1996).

4. Huselid, M. A., Becker, B. E., & Beatty, R. W. (2005). *The workforce scorecard:
    Managing human capital to execute strategy.* Boston, MA: Harvard Business
    Press.

5. Lowenthal, B. D. (2005).Crafting an HR scorecard that works: The ten
    dimensions of an effective measurement system. Retrieved from www.the-
    benchmarkpartners.com.

6. Bucknall, H., & Wei, Z. (2006). *Magic numbers for human resource manage-
    ment: Basic measures to achieve better results.* Hoboken, NJ: John Wiley & Sons.

7. Ulrich, D., Losey, M. R., & Lake, G. (1997). *Tomorrow's HR management: 48
    thought leaders call for change.* Hoboken, NJ: John Wiley & Sons.

8. Kaplan, R. S., & Norton, D. P. (1996).

Chapter 13

1. Mondore, S., & Douthitt, S. (2009). *Investing in what matters: Linking employees to business outcomes.* Alexandria, VA: Society for Human Resource Management.

Appendix A

1. Neither the Society for Human Resource Management nor the authors are compensated in any way from or by SPSS from the authors' recommendation. The authors have used this product over many years and have found it to be reliable and capable of handling critical data and complicated analyses. Secondly, this recommendation is solely the authors' and does not necessarily represent, and should not be interpreted to represent, those of SHRM.

Index

About the Authors

Dr. Scott P. Mondore is a Managing Partner of Strategic Management Decisions (SMD) and has significant experience in the areas of corporate strategy, talent management, measurement, customer experience, and organizational development. He has worked for years in internal management and consulting positions across a variety of industries, including transportation, health care, manufacturing, utilities, and hospitality.

Before co-founding SMD, Dr. Mondore served as the East Region President for Morehead Associates. Before joining Morehead, he worked as a Corporate Strategy Director and Talent Management/Executive Development Director at Maersk, Inc. He also worked as an Employee Relations Manager at UPS, focusing on employee assessment and measurement as well as working as a consultant to large and small organizations in both the private and public sector.

He is the co-author of *Investing in What Matters: Linking Employees to Business Outcomes* and has also published scholarly articles on various topics, including employee turnover, employee safety, coaching, litigation, and leadership. Scott holds the title of Adjunct Professor of Psychology at the University of North Carolina at Charlotte and at the University of Georgia, and has held the same status at Fairleigh Dickinson University.

He has a master's degree and doctorate in applied psychology from the University of Georgia and can be reached at smondore@smdhr.com.

Dr. Shane S. Douthitt is a Managing Partner of Strategic Management Decisions (SMD) and has over 15 years of experience in the areas of measurement, talent management, executive assessment and coaching, and organizational development. He has practical experience across a variety of industries, including banking, manufacturing, utilities, pharmaceuticals, and information technology.

Before co-founding SMD, he was the Senior Vice President of Sales & Products at Morehead Associates. Before joining Morehead, Shane worked as a Human Resources Executive and Leadership Development Executive at Bank of America. Shane also worked as a consultant for Towers Perrin specializing in the design and delivery of integrated human resource systems. Prior to these experiences, Shane worked as a consultant at IBM and held various HR generalist roles.

He is the co-author of *Investing in What Matters: Linking Employees to Business Outcomes* and has published several articles on a variety of topics, including measurement, teams, individual differences and diversity, employee selection, group dynamics, and cultural openness.

He holds a master's degree and doctorate in applied psychology from the University of Georgia, as well as a master's degree in Industrial/Organizational Psychology from the University of Tulsa and can be reached at sdouthitt@smdhr.com.

Dr. Marisa A. Carson is a Senior Consultant with Strategic Management Decisions (SMD). Prior to joining SMD, Marisa worked in various leadership roles across the finance, utilities, and nonprofit industries with Bank of America, Piedmont Natural Gas, and Bowling Green State University. Marisa has extensive experience in the areas of HR data analytics, leadership development and coaching, employee selection and assessment, performance management, and succession planning. Marisa is skilled in implementing evidence-based HR practices that drive organizational change and enhance leadership effectiveness. She holds a master's degree in Industrial/Organizational Psychology and a doctorate in Organizational Science from the University of North Carolina at Charlotte and can be reached at mcarson@smdhr.com.

Acknowledgements

The authors would like to thank the entire publications team at SHRM, particularly Christopher Anzalone, for all of his help throughout this process and the text and cover designer, Shirley Raybuck.

We also would like to thank all of the individuals who generously gave their time to review the manuscript drafts, including our spouses, Connie Mondore, Meggin Douthitt, and A.O. Carson, as well as Karen Stamatiades, Lea Soupata, Jeanie Douthitt, Al Stubblefield and Erin Dry. Finally, we would like to thank the many folks that we have worked with from inside and outside of human resources who truly believe in what they do and constantly focus on improving the function.

Additional
SHRM-Published Books

101 Sample Write-Ups for Documenting
Employee Performance Problems: A
Guide to Progressive Discipline &
Termination
By Paul Falcone

Assessing External Job Candidates
By Jean M. Phillips and Stanley M. Gully

Assessing Internal Job Candidates
By Jean M. Phillips and Stanley M. Gully

Becoming the Evidence-Based Manager:
Making the Science of Management
Work for You
By Gary P. Latham

The Cultural Fit Factor: Creating an
Employment Brand That Attracts,
Retains, and Repels the Right
Employees
By Lizz Pellet

Employment Termination Source Book
By Wendy Bliss and Gene Thornton

The Essential Guide to Federal
Employment Laws
By Lisa Guerin and Amy DelPo

From Hello to Goodbye: Proactive Tips
for Maintaining Positive Employee
Relations
By Christine V. Walters

Got a Minute? The 9 Lessons Every
HR Professional Must Learn to Be
Successful
By Dale J. Dwyer and Sheri A. Caldwell

HR Competencies: Mastery at the
Intersection of People and Business
By Dave Ulrich, Wayne Brockbank,
Dani Johnson, Kurt Sandholtz, and Jon
Younger

Human Resource Essentials: Your Guide
to Starting and Running the HR
Function
By Lin Grensing-Pophal

Investing in What Matters: Linking
Employees to Business Outcomes
By Scott P. Mondore and Shane S.
Douthitt

Leading with Your Heart: Diversity and
Ganas for Inspired Inclusion
By Cari M. Dominguez and Jude
Sotherlund

The Legal Context of Staffing
By Jean M. Phillips and Stanley M. Gully

The Manager's Guide to HR: Hiring,
Firing, Performance Evaluations,
Documentation, Benefits, and
Everything Else You Need to Know
By Max Muller

Performance Appraisal Source Book
By Mike Deblieux

Proving the Value of HR: How and Why
to Measure ROI
By Jack J. Phillips and Patricia Pulliam
Phillips

Rethinking Retention in Good Times
and Bad: Breakthrough Ideas for
Keeping Your Best Workers
By Richard P. Finnegan

Staffing Forecasting and Planning
By Jean M. Phillips and Stanley M. Gully

Staffing to Support Business Strategy
By Jean M. Phillips and Stanley M. Gully

Stop Bullying at Work: Strategies and
Tools for HR and Legal Professionals
By Teresa A. Daniel